1938

This book may be kept

Columbia University
STUDIES IN ENGLISH

THE MIDDLE ENGLISH
PENITENTIAL LYRIC

COLUMBIA
UNIVERSITY PRESS
SALES AGENTS

NEW YORK:
LEMCKE & BUECHNER
30–32 WEST 27TH STREET
LONDON:
HENRY FROWDE
AMEN CORNER, E.C.
TORONTO:
HENRY FROWDE
25 RICHMOND ST., W.

THE MIDDLE ENGLISH
PENITENTIAL LYRIC

A STUDY AND COLLECTION
OF EARLY RELIGIOUS VERSE

BY

FRANK ALLEN PATTERSON, Ph.D.

New York

THE COLUMBIA UNIVERSITY PRESS

1911

Norwood Press
J. S. Cushing Co. — Berwick & Smith Co.
Norwood, Mass., U.S.A.

TO

MY FATHER AND MY MOTHER

This Monograph has been approved by the Department of
English in Columbia University as a contribution to knowledge worthy of publication.

A. H. THORNDIKE,

Secretary.

PREFACE

THE main object of this study was at first the investigation of the relations of the Middle English religious lyric to various other kinds of lyric poetry that were well known in the thirteenth and fourteenth centuries; but as the work advanced it became apparent that the exact provenience of the religious lyric could be shown satisfactorily only by printing a large number of these poems with notes pointing out in detail the sources of general ideas and of specific lines, phrases, and words.   Accordingly the completed monograph has taken the form of a collection of sixty-nine lyrics, with rather extensive notes and an introduction that sums up the results of the more minute study.

Of these poems six are here printed for the first time.[1] The prayer, No. 21, is interesting.   Lydgate's poem, *Timor Mortis Conturbat Me*, No. 38, hitherto unpublished, has much literary quality, and belongs to a class of poems having a curious source.   I am gratified from a study of these *Timor Mortis* lyrics to be able to throw light upon the models that Dunbar used in the *Lament for the Makaris*, for it is clear that he took his refrain and other lines from these popular songs on the fear of death.

The sixty-nine poems as a whole show a deep sincerity and a mystic ardor that give them unquestioned beauty. Such a prayer as that beginning 'Ihesu, mercy! mercy, I cry,' No. 22, well bears the sub-title, *A deuoyt Meditacione*. The paraphrase of the *Ave Maris Stella*, No. 43, to mention but one of many songs to the Virgin, is a beautiful expression of the knightly yet religious chivalry that delighted to honor Mary, 'al in liht I-schrud.'

[1] Nos. 6, 21, 26, 28, 38, 60.

In making this selection of lyrics, I have followed definitions and division lines that are stated in the succeeding pages. But perhaps I should remind the reader at the outset that definitions are all too often inadequate, and that lines of demarcation should never stand out too prominently. The selections printed in this volume include all the poems strictly of the class studied — the penitential lyric. It would be rash indeed to say that no possible lyric has been omitted, for there are a few excluded poems that come very near the border line. Yet I believe that the present collection is practically exhaustive.

It is a pleasure to acknowledge the help I have received in preparing this monograph. To the Reverend John F. Quirk, formerly vice-president of Fordham University, I am indebted for hints in regard to the classification of the Middle English religious lyric. I owe much to his encouragement, and to the assurance he gave me that the arrangement, which I had determined upon, was strictly in accordance with the tenets of the Catholic Church. Miss Helen L. Cohen, my friend and fellow-student, who is now engaged upon a study of the *ballade* for the present series, has given me several references, and has kindly offered suggestions concerning the section upon French influence. Professor Raymond Weeks of Columbia University has read the same section and has given me valuable hints. To Professors Ashley H. Thorndike, Jefferson B. Fletcher, George P. Krapp, Harry M. Ayres, and John Erskine, I am indebted for reading the manuscript. To the last three I am especially grateful for suggestions. It is to Professor William Witherley Lawrence, however, that I owe most. He directed my attention to the Middle English religious lyric, and throughout this study rendered invaluable assistance. While in England he secured copies and rotographs of manuscripts for me. To his kindly interest and friendly encouragement, I owe more than I am able to state.

CONTENTS

INTRODUCTION

I

In making a study of the Middle English religious lyrics —
or rather of a section of these lyrics — it becomes necessary
at the outset to define carefully the limits within which the
study is carried on.   By *Middle English* I mean English literature from the Norman Conquest to Tottel's *Miscellany*.   Perhaps the close of the period should be set earlier in the century,
but for the purposes of this monograph, no clear distinction
can be drawn between the religious poetry of 1500 and that
of 1557 ; the anonymous devotional poetry was all essentially
of the same character, and was little influenced, on the one
hand by the Reformation, or on the other by the Renaissance.
The term *religious* gives little difficulty, though it is well to
remember that *religious lyric* as here used does not include
those lyrical poems of a moralizing tone which became so
prominent in the fifteenth century.   Lyrics on the general
subject of death or the miseries of age, though often religious in
tone, are not essentially devotional, and are therefore excluded.
It is not my purpose to enter here into any detailed discussion
of the many theories regarding the exact meaning of the term,
lyric.   In determining the character of any given poem I have
employed the test used by Palgrave,[1] who wrote: 'Lyrical
has been here held essentially to imply that each Poem shall
turn on some single thought, feeling, or situation.'   We may
dwell upon other characteristics of this form of verse — re-
membering the history of the Provençal lyric, we may insist
on the singing quality of the poems, or we may declare with

---

[1] Preface to the *Golden Treasury*, London, 1861.

Gaston Paris that the term often means 'subjective poetry'; [1] yet we shall come in the end to believe that the one requirement of the lyric is unity, and that this unity must be one of emotion.[2] It is this principle of unity to which I have adhered constantly in trying to determine the general class of poems to be admitted into this collection.

Having segregated all the religious lyrics, we find that it is a far more difficult task to discover a further classification within which these poems shall be distributed according to their true nature. From the time of Warton to the present day, the prevailing method has been to group them by means of external — almost accidental — names, such as *Prayers to God, to Christ*, and *to the Virgin Mary*. But such a classification is at open variance with the conception of the lyric as given above, for the unity of the lyric is not expressed by a title chosen from some convenient external feature of the poem, but by a title which in itself signifies the nature of the emotion that is embodied in the lyric.

That such a division of lyrics as *Prayers to God* must contain poems which differ widely in the kinds of emotion that they express, hardly needs proof; and that such a grouping cannot include all the poems which resemble one another in their emotional characteristics is admirably illustrated by No. 56 in this collection — *A preyer to þe fiue woundes*. In content, this poem is a prayer to Christ, asking that his love may be fixed in the heart of the suppliant. In the notes there is printed a second poem, which is obviously modeled upon this lyric, but with this difference, that Mary has been substituted for Christ and her five joys for the five wounds — yet the emotional quality of the poem remains unchanged. German

[1] On prend quelquefois le mot de poésie lyrique dans le sens de poésie subjective, exprimant des sentiments tout personnels; dans ce sens il exclut nécessairement la plus grande partie de la poésie populaire. *La Littérature Française au Moyen Age*, Paris, 1905, p. 191.

[2] See Erskine, *The Elizabethan Lyric*, New York, 1903, Chapter I, for a further development of this theory.

scholars have likewise classed together all the addresses to
Mary and have called them *Mariengebete*, or have collected the
lyrical and dramatic laments of the Virgin and have called
them *Marienklagen*. In the latter case the classification is
perfectly legitimate, for the title signifies the nature of the
poem; but for the *Mariengebete* no such excuse exists, as a
prayer to Mary may express any one of many religious emotions, — it may be a prayer of confession, a supplication for
mercy, an avowal of reformation, or an expression of mystic
love-longing. In fact, a title more artificial and meaningless
would be hard to find. Such a division has the advantage of
being easy to define, for any one can tell a *Mariengebet;* but,
like the similar classification spoken of above, it fails to reveal
the essential nature of the poem, or the underlying and determining emotion of the poet, and so fails in a most important
requisite, because the lyrical expression of an emotion demands
more than a mere chance-chosen title. A classification that
pays no attention to the lyrical units involved must be un-
satisfactory.

Since the existing method of classification fails to arrange
these poems according to their essential characteristics, and puts
beside one another lyrics of the most diverse emotions, it may
be profitable to approach the subject from a different point of
view, and instead of considering merely external features as a
basis for grouping, to look rather at the internal character of
the poems.

An important fact in the history of religion in Western
Europe during the twelfth and thirteenth centuries was the
growth and spread of mysticism. It is hard to believe that
these poems, arising for the most part directly as a result of
that religious awakening, would not show in almost every line
traces of such influence. As a matter of fact, even the most
trite and conventional of these lyrics, such as poems of confession, indicate in a surprising manner, by chance phrases,
how intimately the new religious ideals had entered into the

life of the people and of their clergy. There is scarcely a poem in this selection that does not give evidence in its thought, in its realistic handling of details, in its expression of self-annihilation, of lively horror of sin, or of passionate love-longing for God, that mysticism, whether accepted by all the writers or not, had yet in every case left its impress upon their minds. Since the religious lyrics in Middle English as a whole are above all else mystic, to mysticism we must look for assistance in determining our classification.

Mysticism, as it developed in Western Europe during the twelfth century, was a reaction against the cold, intellectual tenets of scholasticism. Its fundamental doctrine was an implicit, unquestioning faith that appealed directly to the feelings. Its purpose was a union with God in this earthly life; and its method was extremely plain, for it demanded only a complete, all-absorbing consecration. The constant prayer of the mystics was for a closer walk with God, while their daily life was a practical justification of the Christian faith. Since this absolute devotion needed little theory, mysticism in the twelfth century was essentially a simple method of life, free from all the intricate doctrines of scholasticism. Its main principles may be stated easily.

St. Bernard and his followers declared that the soul in its progress to God passed through three distinct stages. The first was called *purificatio*, in which the soul was purged by penitence from the gross sin in which it had been born, and had lived. In this stage of purification most men spent their lives, 'euer lyk to synne and euer repenting.' It is this first degree of love for God that 'behoues ilk man haue þat wil be safe.' [1] Some, however, attained a more perfect state, and entered the second stage, *illuminatio*, in which their souls reached a higher purity than they had before experienced, and were filled with a longing for God in His beauty. To a very few — a much smaller number than is generally believed —

[1] R. R., I, 53.

it was vouchsafed at times to pass into a third stage, *contemplatio*, where their spirits saw and heard things not lawful to utter.

Mysticism, it should be noticed, was from its inception in closest touch with the Church. It had its very roots in the writings of the Apostles, notably of St. John and St. Paul;[1] and its development, though doubtless influenced by the writings of pagan mystics, was not without the Church, but within it. So, as mysticism spread and developed, it affected the Church from within, but in so slow and orthodox a manner that the change was universally felt only in the more exalted ideals of those who lived the contemplative life, or in the increased sincerity and usefulness of those who lived the active life.

I suggest that the Middle English religious lyrics, since they were written either by mystics themselves, or by poets that had come under the influence of mystic thought and experience, should be grouped according to the different states of mystic progress, or to put it more clearly, according to the three main principles of mystic doctrine. Such a division would have the advantage of including those religious lyrics that are not, at least to us, peculiarly mystic, for mysticism itself included all the doctrines and sacraments of the Church; and so, while this classification would not exclude the humblest and most commonplace of prayers, it would yet have room for the most exalted songs of mystic experience. But because a classification cannot be made strictly according to the different stages of mystic progress, in grouping I would abandon the technical names of these states, and be content to apply the principle without insisting upon too rigid division lines; for, indeed, no system of classifying poems should be too strictly followed out.

In the first large division are grouped those poems that express repentance in its widest sense, as it hardly needs to be said that the essence of the purification stage was the expul-

---

[1] Cf. Inge, *Christian Mysticism*, London, 1899, Lecture II.

sion of sin by penitence, by deep sorrow, 'by weeping sincerely and by wearying heaven with prayers.'[1] In the second division are included those poems which are connected more naturally, perhaps, with mystic belief — such as the songs of love-longing, and certain prayers, especially meditations, which were often composed by the mystics to further their progress in divine love. This second group includes practically all the lyrics outside the first class, for, though mystics that entered the highest state of love were evidently wont to burst into song,[2] for present purposes there can be no distinction drawn between different degrees of love-longing. The two larger divisions, then, of English religious lyric poetry of the Middle Ages are : —

I. Poems of Purification.

II. Poems of Divine Love-longing (including all poems that express emotions peculiar to the states of *illuminatio* and of *contemplatio*).

It is with the first class of poems that this study deals.

Penance, the Church has always held, is the first duty of the sinner. The mystics laid much emphasis upon this sacrament ; St. Bernard declared with the Psalmist that the 'first sacrifice to be made to God is a troubled and contrite heart,'[3] and every mystic treatise affirmed that the chief acts of purification were those connected with penitence. Instead, then, of using *Poems of Purification* as a title for this division of lyrics, I shall use *Penitential Poems*, as being more self-evident in its meaning and more easily limited according to Church doctrines.

The Council of Trent in 1551 acknowledged and defined the Sacrament of Penance [4] as follows : —

[1] Cf. St. Bernard, *Sermones in Cantica Canticorum*, xxxvii, Paris, 1719.

[2] *Richard Rolle*, Horstman, I, 59.

[3] St. Bernard, *Sermones in Cantica Canticorum*, x ; translated by Eales, London, 1896, IV, 51.

[4] *The Canons and Decrees of the Sacred and Œcumenical Council of Trent.* Translated by the Reverend J. Waterworth, London [1848], pp. 92–96.

7

But because God, rich in mercy, knows our frame, He hath bestowed a remedy of life even on those who may, after baptism, have delivered themselves up to the servitude of sin and the power of the Devil — the sacrament, to wit, of Penance, by which the death of Christ is applied to those who have fallen after baptism.

Session XIV, chapter I.

It further declared : —

The acts of the penitent, himself, to wit, *contrition, confession,* and *satisfaction,* are, as it were, the matter of this sacrament. Which acts, inasmuch as they are, by God's institution, required in the penitent for the integrity of the sacrament and for the full and perfect remission of sins, are for this reason called the parts of penance.

Session XIV, chapter III.

Contrition, which holds the first place amongst the aforesaid acts of the penitent, is a sorrow of mind, and a detestation for sin committed, with the purpose of not sinning for the future. . . . Wherefore the holy Synod declares that this contrition contains not only a cessation from sin, and the purpose and the beginning of a new life, but also a hatred of the old.

Session XIV, chapter IV.

And as to that imperfect contrition, which is called attrition, because that it is commonly conceived either from the consideration of the turpitude of sin, or from the fear of hell and of punishment, It declares . . . that it is even a gift of God.

Session XIV, chapter IV.

Penance then consists of three parts : *contrition, confession,* and *satisfaction.* The last, *satisfaction,* which consists of the 'acceptance and accomplishment of certain penitential works, in atonement of the sin confessed,'[1] obviously cannot concern us here, and may be dismissed. Contrition, the Council declared, consists of (1) a sorrow for sin ; (2) a purpose of amendment, together with a hatred of the old life. It also stated that imperfect contrition, or attrition, under which men ordinarily repent, arises from the 'consideration of the turpitude of sin, or from the fear of hell and of punishment.' Confession is a declaration of sin before an approved priest, either in public or private.

[1] *The New International Encyclopædia,* New York, s.v. Penance.

This very full and accurate definition of the Sacrament of Penance was not new to the Church when the Council of Trent promulgated it in 1551. The Lateran Council in 1215 had ordered laymen to confess at least once a year, and in the literature of the later Middle Ages constant references to the Parts of Penance are found. Dante was familiar with the doctrine, and English literature abounds in references to identical conceptions — as witness Chaucer's Parson, who declares that 'contricioun is the verray sorwe that a man receyveth in his herte for his synnes, with sad purpos to shryve hym and to do penaunce, and neveremoore to do synne.'[1] Likewise, the Prymer of Salisbury begins a short treatise on Confession in these words : —

'Fyrst : What is penitence?

Penitence is the emendacyon of the lyfe, with inwarde contricyon of hert for the synne committed : with a full purpose never to do the synne agayn.'[2]

Applying this definition of penance, as it was fully stated in the acts of the Council of Trent, to the classification of the penitential lyrics, we find that they fall naturally into two classes. In the first group are those poems which express a confession of sin;[3] in the second, those in which the emotion is that of contrition. This latter class is further divided into two groups : poems expressing a sorrow for sin, and poems expressing a desire for amendment.

In the practical application of these theories of classification, as has been said, it must be borne in mind at every point that the lines of demarcation must not be drawn too rigidly. The lyric in itself involves unity of emotion. It is the nature of this unit as a whole, not of single detached elements of this unit, that must finally determine the classification of a poem.

[1] *The Parson's Tale*, ll. 127–130.

[2] Maskell, *Monumenta Ritualia*, London, 1846, II, p. 271.

[3] For reasons of simplicity, I have in grouping placed *confession* before *contrition*.

To illustrate, confessions early in the thirteenth century or before took conventionalized forms in which the main element was a rehearsal of sins; but the fact that a sinner enumerates his sins implies contrition on his part as the cause of such enumeration. It would be strange indeed if expressions of this fundamental cause — a sorrow for sin — did not at times enter into the strictest of confessions. And so in the first poem, *A General Confession*, there are lines which plainly indicate contrition. Again, take No. 22. In this poem we have an acknowledgment of the seven deadly sins, and other elements that come directly from liturgical confessions, yet the scribe was clearly right in calling the prayer 'a deuoyt Meditacione'; for there is no poem in this collection that in its entirety gives so complete an expression of a contrite and sorrowing sinner. Thus David, in what is perhaps the most perfect example of a contrition poem ever written, finds occasion to say, 'I acknowledge my transgressions, and my sin is ever before me.' In truth, it is hard to conceive of a man as expressing a real deeply felt sorrow for sin, without incidentally mentioning the sins for which he is penitent.

So it must be remembered, that, though the parts of penance were clearly established in the minds of medieval Christians, in the classification of penitential poems the boundary lines are not fast and firm, but are ever fluctuating; since in its very nature, confession implies contrition, and contrition implies at least something of confession. The Council had indeed said as much as this, for it declared that there are three principal emotions in the mind of the penitent — confession of sin, sorrow for sin, and a desire for amendment. We shall find, therefore, that all these emotions may enter into a penitential lyric, and yet not destroy its perfect unity. It is the predominance of one emotion that must determine the emotional unity of the poem, and hence, its classification.

This grouping has little of the rigidity that it appears to assume when presented in outline as hereafter. The chief value of the definitions gained from the Council of Trent lies in the fact that they give us a firm basis for determining what constitutes a penitential lyric. If by using these definitions we are able to group the lyrics among themselves, and so, by psychological principles, to place in proximity poems of like nature, it is desirable; but it must always be distinctly understood that such a grouping is entirely tentative and suggestive, and by no means inevitable.

A few words further in regard to the practical application of this scheme will not be out of place. A confession, as I have considered it, is a poem in which the main emotion is an acknowledgment of sin. The confessions based upon the liturgy furnish the standard. These I have divided into two classes, public and extended confessions. The public confession is the *confiteor* that was used in all the Western churches during the time in which these poems were written. It consisted of two parts: the confession proper, in which acknowledgment of sin was made; and the prayer for intercession with which it closed.[1] So in any confession poem the main element is a declaration of sin; but at the same time a prayer for forgiveness and mercy, corresponding to the prayer for intercession, is natural, and strictly in agreement with the model *confiteor*. Extended confessions are a further development of liturgical forms. They are found in English as well as in Latin prose. They are most frequent in the Prymers, where they were evidently used as private devotions. They are usually, though not necessarily, addressed directly to the Divinity, and consist of a detailed rehearsal of sins, covering the ten commandments, the five wits, the seven deadly sins, and other conventional enumerations of error and wrongdoing.[2]

Other confessions have the same general emotion as the liturgical poems; but the acknowledgment of sin is less formal,

[1] See the note to No. 1 for a model confession.
[2] See the note to No. 3 for a typical extended confession.

while the prayer for mercy is likely to occupy a more prominent part, appearing often in every stanza.

Contrition poems are those in which the main feeling is
(1) a sorrow for sin or (2) a purpose of amendment. The emotion of the first class of these poems may arise from a 'consideration of the turpitude of sin or from a fear of hell and of
punishment.' Hence, we infer that a contrition poem may
deal with past sins; in this form of prayer the sinner loathes
his infirmities, and calls out to God for pardon and mercy.[1]
Or a contrition poem may express little of what is usually
considered sorrow for sin, as the poet becomes more and more
concerned with a fear of the future judgment in his typical
cry, 'Loverd, shyld me vrom helle deth.' [2]

The second group of contrition poems — I do not care to
say *division*, for the line of separation is not marked, neither
is it necessarily fundamental — consists of poems in which the
main emotion is a purpose of amendment, stated or implied.
Hence, in this second group, the poems deal principally with the
future earthly life, not as in the first group, with the past life
or the future judgment. Sometimes, as in No. 49, the poet
resolves definitely to reform. More often, however, the penitent prays that in the future he may do no more deadly sin,
and that he may have Heaven's protection from harm and the
wiles of the devil.

It may seem that the distinction between these two groups
of contrition poems is too slight to justify a separation. Since
in grouping poems within a large division, it is desirable to
place near each other pieces of identical emotion, so long as we
keep within the large class, we may group as the emotion seems
to indicate, without, however, establishing too sharp division
lines. By comparing a typical poem of the former group with
one from the latter group it will be at once apparent that the
two subdivisions are fairly distinct, and that, were the line of

---

[1] The typical example of this group of contrition poems is found in the fifty-
first Psalm, before mentioned.   [2] No. 11.

division withdrawn, we should have poems of unlike nature in close proximity. Take for instance, the first lines of No. 22 : —

> Ihesu, mercy! mercy, I cry:
>   myn vgly synnes þou me forgyfe.
> Þe werlde, my flesch, þe fende, felly
>   þai me besale both strange & styfe;
> I hafe ful oft to þaim consent,
>   & so to do it is gret drede;
> I ask mercy with gud entent;
>   Ihesu, mercy for my mysdede !

Throughout this poem the predominating emotion is a sorrow for sin, for the poet is thinking almost entirely of his past life and of the future judgment. Compare with this poem the Lord's Prayer, either in the translations or the paraphrases,[1] and it will be seen that the main emotion is always a desire to be kept from sin and to be helped in this present earthly life. Thus the original of the poems reads: 'Thy kingdom come: thy will be done in earth as it is in heaven; give us this day our daily bread. . . . Lead us not into temptation, but deliver us from evil.' It is obvious that, although the poems of the two groups have elements in common, — for the Lord's prayer has the petition, 'Forgive us our trespasses,' — to place together poems as unlike as are the typical ones compared above, is to introduce needless confusion and to disregard their real nature.

I have elsewhere treated the indebtedness of many of these lyrics to the liturgy; accordingly I have subdivided each large group into liturgical and non-liturgical lyrics; and I have further tried to group poems of a like nature by placing together all lyrics with similar titles, when such poems have a common underlying emotion.

---

[1] Such, for instance, as No. 40.

Classification of Penitential Lyrics

A. Poems of Confession.
  I. Liturgical.
    a. Public.
      (1) 1. A General Confession.
      (2) 2. A Form of Confession.
    b. Extended.
      (3) 1. General Confession of Sins.
      (4) 2. A Confessioun to Ihesu crist.
  II. Non-Liturgical.
    a. Informal.
      (5) 1. As I wandrede her bi weste.
      (6) 2. I wite my self myne owne woo.
      (7) 3. A Prayer to our Lady.
      (8) 4. Heȝe louerd, þou here my bone.
      (9) 5. God þat al þis myhtes may.
B. Poems Expressing Contrition.
  α. Sorrow for Sin.
    I. Liturgical.
      a. Paraphrases and Translations of Portions of Services.
        (10) 1. The Prayer.
        (11) 2. Loverd, Shyld Me vrom Helle Deth.
        (12) 3. In Manus Tuas.
        (13) 4. To our Lady.
      b. Poems Built upon the Litany.
        (14) 1. Prey We to the Trinyte.
      c. Other Poems Showing Strong Liturgical Influence.
        (15) 1. A Short Prayer after the Levation for Mercy.
        (16) 2. A preyer at þe leuacioun.
        (17) 3. Ihesu, Fili Dei, Miserere Me.
        (18) 4. Prayer for God's Mercy.
        (19) 5. Prayer to Mary.
        (20) 6. Prayer to St. Elene.
        (21) 7. Deus in nomine tuo saluum me fac.

II. Non-Liturgical.
    a. Prayers to the Deity.
        (22) 1. Ihesu, Mercy for my Mysdede !
        (23) 2. An orisoun to vr lord Ihesu.
        (24) 3. Ihesu Criste, haue mercy one me.
        (25) 4. her biginneþ an orisun of þe trinite.
        (26) 5. Do mercy to fore thi jugement.
        (27) 6. Iesu crist, heouene kyng.
        (28) 7. To The, Maist Peirlas Prince of Pece.
    b. Poems to the Virgin Mary.
        (29) 1. Hail, Mary !
        (30) 2. Hymn of the Virgin.
        (31) 3. An Orison to our Lady.
        (32) 4. A Song to the Virgin.
        (33) 5. Nou skrinkeþ rose & lylie flour.
    c. Timor Mortis Poems.
        (34) 1. The best Song as hit semeth me.
        (35) 2. Evere more, where so euer I be.
        (36) 3. In what estate so euer I be.
        (37) 4. Alas, my hart will brek in thre.
        (38) 5. Timor Mortis Conturbat Me.
β. Prayers to Be Kept from Sin, and for Aid.
  I. Liturgical.
    a. Translations and Paraphrases.
        (39) 1. Pater Noster in Anglico.
        (40) 2. Pater Noster.
        (41) 3. Hymn to God.
        (42) 4. Heyl, levedy, se-stoerre bryht.
        (43) 5. A Prayer to the Virgin Mary.
        (44) 6. Come, Shuppere, Holy Gost.
        (45) 7. A Prayer for Grace.
        (46) 8. To þe gude angell.
  II. Non-Liturgical.
    a. Resolves to Reform.
        (47) 1. A Resolve to Reform.

b. General Prayers to the Deity for Protection from Sin.
- (48) 1. A Morning Thanksgiving and Prayer to God.
- (49) 2. An Orisoun to god.
- (50) 3. Mane Nobiscum, Domine !
- (51) 4. Prayer for the Seven Gifts of the Holy Ghost.

c. Prayers to Christ.
- (52) 1. Oratio magistri Richardi de castre, quam ipse posuit.
- (53) 2. Hymn to Jesus Christ.
- (54) 3. Alya Cantica.
- (55) 4. An Orisoun to þe fyue Woundes of iesu cristus.
- (56) 5. A preyer to þe fiue woundes.
- (57) 6. Invocation to the Cross.

d. Prayers to the Virgin Mary.
- (58) 1. Godric's Song to the Virgin.
- (59) 2. To the Virgin Mary.
- (60) 3. Oracio ad Sanctam Mariam.
- (61) 4. A preiere to vre ladi.
- (62) 5. Another Prayer to the Virgin Mary.
- (63) 6. An orisoun to the fyue ioyes of vre lady.
- (64) 7. Hymn to the Virgin.
- (65) 8. Iblessed beo þu, Lauedi.
- (66) 9. Seinte Marie, Moder Milde.
- (67) 10. An orison to vr lady.
- (68) 11. The Five Joys of the Virgin.
- (69) 12. Hymn to the Virgin.

II

This monograph does not attempt to study the early history of the Middle English lyric, or to give a mere repetition of facts already many times told and readily accessible. No attempt then will be made to sketch the chronological development of the vernacular lyric.[1]   The problems with which the remainder of this study has to deal are two : first a consideration of the conditions of medieval English life which brought about this apparently sudden growth of the vernacular religious lyric ; and secondly, a study of the literary influences that affected the poems printed in the present volume.

It is probable that the Middle English religious lyric did not develop so quickly as the few early poems that have survived might lead us to believe.   Extant specimens of religious lyrics in Anglo-Saxon prove that the vernacular was sometimes used in this kind of verse.[2]   There are references in the Latin chroniclers, also, that sustain the point.   Particularly interesting is the account which William of Malmesbury[3] gives of Aldhelm,[4] who used to stand on a bridge, singing secular ditties till he had gained the attention of passers-by, when he began gradually to introduce religious ideas into his songs.

During the years preceding the Norman Conquest as well as during the century following it, the practice of singing religious songs in the vernacular can hardly have been uncommon.   It

[1] There is no good history of the Middle English lyric.   Ten Brink's account in his *History of English Literature*, though slight, is the most satisfactory. Something will be found in other histories of Middle English literature, though as a rule such accounts are of little value, for the main interest of the writers of general histories lies in other fields, such as romances and tales.   Of the special studies, Mr. E. K. Chambers's essay, in Chambers and Sidgwick's *Early English Lyrics*, is enlightening; he deals especially with the origin of the lyric. In this connection should be mentioned two notable studies by French scholars on the origin of the French lyrics — A. Jeanroy, *Les Origines de la Poésie lyrique en France au Moyen Age*, Paris, 1892; and Gaston Paris's review of the same in the *Journal des Savants*, 1892.   For the later lyrics, Professor Padelford's Chapter on *Transition Song Collections*, in the *Cambridge History of English Literature*, should be mentioned; his introduction to the *Early Sixteenth Century Lyrics* is also excellent.   The field of the Middle English lyric is interesting in many ways; I hope some time to write an account of the development of this vernacular verse.

[2] Cf. Grein und Wülker, *Bibliothek der angelsächsischen Poesie*, II, 211 ff.

[3] *De Gest. Pontif. Angl.* Lib. V, Pars prima, in Migne, *Patrologiæ*, 179, 1621.

[4] Aldhelm died in 709.

is only from the latter part of the twelfth century, however, that the earliest extant religious vernacular lyrics date. St. Godric, who died in 1170, wrote three short English poems. In these songs are found all the essential qualities of later lyrics — the mysticism, the expression of divine love in terms of worldly affection, and to a slight extent, the liturgical origin of phrases. A little later the *Poema Morale* [1] and *On God Ureisun of ure Lefdi* [2] were written. It is impossible from this time to trace with accuracy the history of the English religious lyric. Poetry as a means of religious instruction or as a mode for expressing divine emotion became popular in a manner that was doubtless unknown in England before. Every kind of religious feeling found expression in verse; prayers fell naturally into rhyme, and sermons took the likeness of poetry. Friars found it convenient to set forth in easily remembered verse the simple teachings of the faith, and monks in their monasteries turned irresistibly in their adoration for Mary to expression in song; even the lonely hermit having reached the glories of a union with God, exclaimed, 'þe sange of louyng & of lufe es commen.' [3]

Yet with all this verse-making there existed much doubt of its real religious value; for, when friars, monks, clerks, and even laymen took to numbers, it was doubtless time to consider if the arch-fiend were not sometimes to be detected therein working out his own designs. For this reason Richard Rolle hastened to explain in regard to the songs which he had previously declared a convert might sing while in the third degree of love, 'nogth bodyly cryand with þe mouth — of þat maner of syngyn speke I nogth, ffor þat sang has bath gud and ille.' [4]

[1] The *Poema Morale* is not strictly speaking a lyric, but rather a sermon in lyrical verse. The consensus of opinion seems to be that the oldest MSS. date from the late twelfth century. See Anna C. Paues, *A Newly Discovered MS. of the Poema Morale*, Anglia, xxx, 217.

[2] Cotton. MS. Nero A xiv; printed, Morris, E. E. T. S., 34, 191.

[3] Richard Rolle, in *The Form of Perfect Living*, R. R., I, 32.

[4] *Form of Perfect Living*, R. R., I, 33.

c

18

A proper precaution, indeed, but in view of Rolle's own habit, even in this treatise, not so very convincing. A hundred years before this the holy St. Edmund had felt some compunction on the general subject of prayers in verse, and had made bold to say, 'þerefore he doþ gret schome and gret vnreuerrence to god þat takeþ him to Rymede wordes & queynte, and leueþ þe wordes and þe preyere þat he vs tauhte.'[1] The saint, however, did not actually think it such 'foul lechery to delyten in such Rymynge' as one might conclude, for he himself made several lyrics in 'turned langage and rymed,' one of which is represented in this volume.[2]

Thus it was that during the thirteenth century there were written many religious lyrics — how many, we can judge by the large number yet preserved in spite of the ravages of the Reformation, and by the constant references in didactic treatises to these poems of divine love and devotion. Though it is impossible to give anything like an adequate history of the beginning of this religious poetry, it is possible to study the influences that were at work, and from such a study to draw in large outline a description of the conditions out of which this kind of religious verse in England developed.

The religious lyric in England before 1200 had found complete expression in Latin. In this language were written the hymns that were used in the Church services as well as much poetry of private devotion. During the twelfth and thirteenth centuries, however, a tendency that had been present in the Church from its very foundation came to be a prominent part of its life. Mysticism took a commanding place in religious thought and experience in England. The main doctrines of the mystics have been mentioned already and need not be repeated. This system of belief worked out in two distinct directions, paradoxically opposite. The first tendency of the mystic was perhaps toward isolation; he naturally sought to remove himself from the world and to find in seclu-

[1] *The Mirror of St. Edmund*, R.R., I, 251. [2] No. 23.

sion the blessedness of a union with God. It was thus that St. Godric and Richard Rolle found the rewards of a lonely contemplative life exceeding precious.

But there was another side to religious life, even as led by mystics. Since it had been recorded of the founder of mysticism that he went about doing good, his followers of the twelfth century remembered well his example. Even Richard Rolle, though declaring that the contemplative life is higher than the active, urges his friends not to enter it hastily, but rather to remain in the humbler station. His own example in rendering the Psalms and in writing for the laity shows his sincerity. It is this second, practical tendency of the mystic movement that is most interesting to the student of the religious lyric. The result of the development of mysticism in England was an awakening of the Church, and a widespread revival of religion that causes the period to be called to-day by writers on the history of the Church, 'The thirteenth, greatest of centuries.'[1] Under the impelling love of God, which mysticism had aroused, there were written tracts, homilies, legends, and poems whose purpose was to create in the ignorant laity a deep religious life.[2] So it came about that, though Latin was retained in the formal Church services as preserving more perfectly the dignity and reverential awe suitable to public worship, the vernacular came into use for the more practical purposes of the active life. From using the common language for the purpose of religious teaching, it was but a step to expressing that teaching in poetical form, always more pleasing to the popular ear, and more easily remembered. It is not strange, then, that among the early Middle English religious lyrics are found versified renderings of the *Pater Noster* and Creed. The missionary spirit, the practical side of mysticism, was the leading motive in the development of the vernacular religious lyric. This phase of mysticism accounts

[1] The reference is to Dr. J. J. Walsh's recent book of the same name.
[2] Cf. Horstman in the Introduction to *Richard Rolle of Hampole*, I, xii–xiii.

in part for the large number of liturgical lyrics found in this volume. Not that Latin poems were no longer written, — they were produced in abundance, — but the selfish desire to write in a language understood only by the clerks was no longer supremely attractive; literary art was sacrificed to religious devotion; and the ignorant laity were taught in simple, homely words the mysteries of the faith.

Another influence that helped to develop the English religious lyric was the vogue of the *chansons* in France. While all England was being stirred by this deep religious awakening, there came the knowledge that poets across the Channel were singing songs of worldly love in their native tongue. The English had always had a peculiar love for the Holy Virgin, a love that mysticism had intensified into an ardent adoration. It needed only a hint from France to cause this enthusiasm to burst forth. So it is that among the earliest Middle English lyrics are some that are liturgical and some that sing in glowing terms of divine love.

The principal influences, then, that brought about this development of English religious verse were, first, the missionary spirit of mysticism; and secondly, the custom in France of singing songs of worldly love in the spoken language. Furthermore, the literary influences that affected these lyrics were likewise of two kinds — Latin and French.

III

The influence of Latin upon the Middle English religious lyric comes from two main sources, the liturgy and patristic writings. Of these two influences, that of the liturgy is far more important; the influence of the sermons and treatises of the Fathers is comparatively slight. The actual sources of the early vernacular religious lyric lie, in most cases, in the words of the services of the Church — words that were read, sung, and prayed, not daily only, but often several times daily.

It will not be amiss to consider in some detail the various ways in which the religious poet turned the liturgy to the uses of lyric verse.

The intimate relation between the liturgy and the vernacular lyric in England is seen most obviously, perhaps, in the large number of metrical translations. As already stated, the clerks, in their anxiety to make the ways of salvation clear and open to the ignorant, and at the same time attractive and easily remembered, often rendered the more important portions of the services into rhymed verse.

The Public Confession, which was used by the people before the Mass, was often rendered in verse, sometimes with faithful accuracy, more often merely paraphrased. The Extended Confessions, which seldom were used in the formal services, but which are found in almost all the Prymers, were frequently rhymed, sometimes doubtless for the devotion of the poet himself, but far more often to serve as the private confession to God of the unlettered laity. There is a conventional spirit about these poems that seldom allows them to become subjective; even in Dunbar, the missionary spirit is easily read between the lines, for such a study as the present one reveals clearly that, in spite of the statements of editors, the poet is making no serious personal admissions.

The Lord's Prayer was particularly popular with metrical translators. Paraphrases also of this prayer were often made. Still more noticeable is the widespread habit of embedding the *Pater Noster* entire in a religious lyric where we should hardly expect it to occur. Other prayers were often rendered in verse. When the translator of the York *Hours* came to the long Prayer he instinctively turned from prose to poetry. The liturgical prayer, *In Manus Tuas*, was constantly put into vernacular verse for the daily use of the devout.

The antiphons, responses, and versicles were often rendered into poetry. Thus, the poem, *Loverd, Shyld Me vrom Helle Deth*, No. 11, is an almost literal translation of the response and versicles following the ninth lesson in the *Offices of the Dead*. *To þe gude angell*, No. 46, is a rendering of a portion of the *Office of the Proper Angel*, according to the use of Sarum. The many poems that celebrate the joys of the Virgin go back ultimately to certain antiphons in the *Horae*. Sometimes the paraphrase is fairly close, but often, as in Nos. 63 and 68, the resemblance is not marked; of the ultimate origin of this class of poems, however, there can be no doubt.[1]

Portions of scripture, especially the seven penitential Psalms, were often versified. No. 21 is an interesting translation and expansion of Psalm 53. Very often some incident related in the Bible forms the basis for a poem. Thus No. 17, *Ihesu, Fili Dei, Miserere Mei*, is founded upon Christ's visit into the coasts of Tyre and Sidon, as told in Matthew 15 : 21–22. No. 50, *Mane Nobiscum, Domine*, tells of the walk to Emmaus, and adapts the words of Caiphas, *Dwell with us, Lord*, as a prayer suitable for all Christians.

Some of the hymns of the Church were rendered into English, yet not so many as one might suppose. Friar Herebert is the translator of the only hymns found in this volume — the *Ave Maris Stella* and *Veni Creator Spiritus*. The note attached to the manuscript poems implies that they were frequently used for devotional purposes: 'Qui usum hujus quaterni habuerit, oret pro anima dicti fratris.' But after all, since hymns were not indispensable to the spiritual welfare of the common people, it need cause no surprise that so few of them were put into vernacular verse.[2] A late paraphrase of the *Ave Maris Stella* forms one of the most beautiful poems among the Middle English religious lyrics, but it is not a typical rendering, either in its purpose, which is far from missionary, or in its emotion, which is largely subjective.

Closely related to the paraphrases are a number of poems that take their subjects from lines in the services. Thus,

[1] Cf. No. 63, 14, note.
[2] There are, of course, some translated hymns still unprinted.

upon a single prominent liturgical thought, a writer will often develop a unified poem. A line from the response after the eighth lesson in the *Offices of the Dead* furnished the theme for many Middle English lyrics — the *Timor Mortis* poems. No. 34, likewise, employs almost all the original response, incorporating the Latin lines, not as refrains, but as integral parts of the poem. No. 28 makes use of the liturgical line, *Miserere mei, deus*, as a text in the form of a refrain.

A number of poems take the litany as a foundation. No. 14 is little else than an invocation after the manner of the litany; No. 13 forms one of several prayers to various divine personages; and No. 4 closes with the litany.

Some poems, though they have no direct source in the services, are evidently modeled after liturgical prayers or were made for use during worship. *A preyer at þe leuacioun*, No. 16, is sufficiently explained by its title. Such prayers seem to have been widely used during the Mass.[1] The first lines of No. 15, *A Short Prayer after the Levation for Mercy*, give an idea of these poems : —

> Lord, als þou can, & als þou wille,
> haue mercy of me, þat has don ille;
> for what-so þou wiþ me wil do,
> I holde me payde to stonde þer-to.

This poem probably had no direct original in any order of the Mass, yet were it not found in the *Lay Folks' Mass Book* there were no proof needed to show its liturgical origin. The prayers to Mary, No. 19, and to St. Elene, No. 20, likewise suggest liturgical nature and use.

The influence of the liturgy upon these poems is felt in more ways, however, than in mere translations and paraphrases; the most important contribution of the services was in the countless words, phrases, and ideas that they gave to the poets, and from which these writers, in many cases, derived the very

[1] See No. 15, note.

subject-matter and expression of their songs. 'Lord, make me safe,' prays the poet again and again, as he recalls the words of the Psalmist that formed a part of the sublime response, *Peccantem me quotidie . . . Deus . . . salvum me fac*. Not this response alone, but the entire *Office of the Dead*, partly in the various prayers and versicles, partly in the lessons from the *Book of Job*, has contributed largely to the penitential lyrics. 'Lord, despise nouȝht þe wark of þin handes,' beseeches the poet, translating the response: *Opera manuum tuarum, Domine, ne despicas*. Or again he pleads, "Damn not that þou dere has bouȝht," which inevitably suggests the prominent versicle: *Nunc, Christe, te petimus miserere, quæsumus; qui venisti redimere perditos, noli damnare redemptos*. The *Hymn to the Virgin*, No. 30, is a mosaic of phrases and ideas borrowed from the hymns, prayers, responses, versicles, lessons, and scripture found in the *Horae*.

Not only did the liturgy furnish most of the prominent and striking thoughts found in these poems, but it furnished in abundance the most commonplace expressions. The conception, for instance, that Christ bought the world with his blood, shed upon the cross, is only one of many ideas that formed the body of the liturgy. From thence, where they were repeated daily and even hourly, these ideas were transferred to the lyrics, often with identity of language, and constantly used.

Aside from these passages, which show much minute borrowing in thought and phrase from the services of the Church, the medieval poets seem to have taken from the liturgy certain peculiar ways of looking at life. The custom of thinking of sin as a disease, of the sinner as a sufferer, and of Christ as the physician, found expression in the Gospels, and was often used in the liturgy, especially in the Mass, whence it was probably taken in most instances by the poet, rather than from any patristic source. The realistic manner in which death is always considered doubtless owes more to the lessons in the *Offices of the Dead* than to any other influence.

It has been assumed by many scholars that the Middle English religious lyric owes much to the Latin hymns and to sacred Latin poetry. In the matter of metrical form such may be the case, but in content the English lyrics in this volume owe nothing to the sacred Latin lyric, and but little to the Latin hymns. No. 30, as mentioned above, was indebted partly to Church hymns, as well as to liturgical prayers, responses, and lessons; there are also two translations of Latin hymns in this collection. Only thus far are the lyrics here printed related to the hymns of the Church; and it should be pointed out that in No. 30 the parallels came directly from the services, for the poet knew his *Horae* most thoroughly, as passages taken from other parts of it show; and that of the two translated hymns, both were necessary parts of almost every service. What influence the Latin hymns had upon the content of these lyrics came invariably through the liturgy; so far as I can determine after a careful reading of the fifty-one volumes of the *Analecta hymnica* [1] and other collections of sacred Latin poetry, Latin hymns and devotional Latin poetry had no appreciable influence upon the development of the Middle English religious lyric.

It was the liturgy that generally suggested the subject-matter of these poems. From it the writers took their words, their phrases, their sentences, their ideas — the very content of their poems. It is not strange; for, if out of the fullness of the heart the mouth speaketh, surely the thirteenth century monks and clerks were amply justified in using the liturgy as their foundation; indeed, they could not have done otherwise. The full indebtedness of these poems to the services cannot be realized until a careful comparison between them and the liturgy has been made, phrase with phrase and thought with thought. It is only by detailed study that such influence can be shown; its

[1] Dreves, *Analecta hymnica medii aevi*, Leipzig, 1886–1910, Vols. 1–51, in progress.

full extent is best seen in the many parallel passages cited in the notes.

It has already been implied that the Middle English religious lyric is peculiarly free from all theological doctrines. The abstract and scholarly reasoning of Lanfranc and Anselm was far removed from the simple faith and humble devotion of the religious poets. Likewise, the intricate and over-subtle logic of medieval philosophers found no echo either in the lives or writings of these devoted clerks. Mysticism, as it developed under St. Bernard, was a protest and a reaction against scholasticism; and these poems, which, as before stated, constitute one of the direct results of the mystic movement, are at all times conspicuously free from abstract theology. Even the more learned of the mystic writers seem to have had little influence; Lanfranc, Anselm, and Hugo of St. Victor undoubtedly affected a few of the earlier pieces in prose and verse,[1] but their influence is not felt upon the lyrics here printed. The penitential lyric was extremely simple in every aspect; its purpose was practical, and its methods direct. Even in the songs to Mary, where the missionary spirit is not so obvious, the writers show little sympathy with intricate and subtle logic; mysticism was in the air, and mysticism, in its purpose at least, was plain, direct, fervent, — a matter of the heart, not of the intellect. The interesting question, *Cur Deus homo*, found little response in the imaginations of unlearned men, who accepted without hesitation the fundamental truth of Christianity; for them the simple doctrines of the liturgy were enough, for in these, indeed, they found the words of life.

But the Fathers were not always intricate and subtle in their writings. St. Anselm was truly regarded as an earnest and devout man. His prayers and meditations were filled with the noble sincerity of his life. Yet even his simple devotions do not seem to find a single echo in these lyrics; though well

[1] Cf. W. Vollhardt, *Einfluss der Lateinischen Geistlichen Litteratur auf Einige Kleinere Schöpfungen der Englischen Übergangsperiode*, Leipzig, 1888.

known to priests in higher orders, they were evidently not so widely disseminated among the clerks and humbler servants of the Church. Although the higher clergy, less closely in touch with the common people, allowed themselves to refer to learned doctrines with which they were constantly familiar, and which their sophisticated readers would readily understand, they did not incorporate them in English poetry, for they composed in nothing less dignified than Latin or French. Robert Grosseteste wrote the allegorical *Castle of Love* in French verse, and even St. Edmund composed several poems in this language, though none in English. Most of the vernacular religious lyrics were written by friars and monks, who naturally used not only the material best suited to their practical needs and devotional purposes, but also that with which they were most familiar. It was left to them to express in plain yet attractive language the great truths of the Church.

Of the two or three writers who affected in any way the content of the penitential lyric, St. Edmund, who has been mentioned already, had by far the most considerable influence. His earnest and unquestioned piety had been richly expressed in his *Speculum Ecclesiæ*. Edmund died in 1240, and was canonized in 1246.[1] The *Mirror* became immediately popular, and was translated into French and English many times during the two succeeding centuries. There was hardly a monastery without a copy; it was one of those books that precede public thought. England was at that time approaching the full development of mysticism. St. Edmund's *Mirror* was just in advance of the age; it was filled with a mystic fire and devotion that appealed to Richard Rolle and his followers, for in it they found many of their ideas. With the spread of mysticism the *Speculum* became almost a handbook of religious devotion, and as such it was often rendered into simple English prose for the use of the unlearned.

[1] There is no adequate modern life of St. Edmund. A good bibliographical account of the material extant is given in the *Dictionary of National Biography*.

There is no single writer who exercised such widespread influence upon the religious lyrics of England as did St. Edmund. No. 26, *Do mercy to fore thi Jugement*, probably is indebted to the *Mirror* for one entire stanza and for various other passages. No. 48 is a rendering of prayers found in the *Speculum*, and a development of devotions suggested by the saint. Other poems show in slighter ways how greatly the *Mirror* had affected the religious thought and emotions of the English people. St. Edmund also wrote a poem in French verse that was admirably translated in *An orisoun to or lord Ihesu*, No. 23.

One of St. Edmund's disciples was Richard Rolle. Two or three poems in this collection are almost certainly the work of Rolle; in other lyrics there are a spirit and atmosphere that are peculiar to the later mystics. Undoubtedly Rolle and his followers influenced these poems more than can now be determined.

Philosophers did not always write beyond the comprehension of common men; at times, like St. Anselm, they became exceedingly simple in their devotions. St. Thomas of Aquinas was a man who added to a reputation for remarkable acuteness in reasoning and in making subtle deductions, a devout and humble mind. He composed several prayers in Latin, one of which, because of its expression of a complete and earnest consecration, became immediately well known throughout the Church. It was translated and retranslated as a practical example of a fervent prayer. In its short lines and repeated grammatical constructions it easily lent itself to verse. No. 49, *an Orisoun to god*, is a literal translation of this prayer in rhymed couplets.

The influence of other mystic writers is seen in these poems only indirectly. Thoughts that ultimately originated with St. Bernard are found in the last poem in the volume, but it is altogether unlikely that the author of this lyric had ever read the saint's mystic sermons. Some of St. Bernard's ideas became immediately popular in France, and were reiterated by French religious poets, from whom, in all probability, the few and slight parallels were drawn.

The effect of the English sermons does not seem to have been widespread. The *Poema Morale*, a sermon couched in lyric verse, had decided influence upon one lyric, No. 7, *A Prayer to our Lady*. Other poems show traces of the sermons, but in no case do they exhibit any evident connection with homilies at present published. The influence of sermons upon such lyrics as No. 6, *I wite my self myne owne woo*, is certainly greater than at present can be proved.

Such in general was the effect of patristic writings upon the Middle English lyric. The works by which the Fathers earned their scholarly reputations, and by which they influenced and even regulated the lines of theological thought, were unknown to the writers of simple, vernacular verse; it was not until a work had proved of practical help, and had been often translated, that it found its way into the English lyrics.

IV

The French influence found in these poems is derived mainly from the lyric poetry of Northern France. The type which seems to have affected most directly the English religious lyric is that simple love-song, the *chanson d'amour*, which flourished in the thirteenth century and before. This love-lyric consists rarely of more than five stanzas,[1] and often of less, with the rhymes occurring regularly, but with the stanzas not necessarily of the same length, a short verse being often used after one, two, or more long lines.

In content the *chanson d'amour* is well defined. For an introduction it seems to have employed almost invariably one

---

[1] Cf. P. Paris in *Hist. Litt.*, XX, 613 : La chanson est un poëme ordinairement composé de cinq couplets uniformes, destinés à être chantés sur une modulation adaptée à l'expression et à la mesure du premier de ces couplets.

of two conventions. Most frequently the poet, starting with a nature setting, tells how the fresh woods and flowers turn his thought to a lady 'feir and fre,' or the autumn leaves in fading remind him of his grief — a grief, however, *tres douce*.[1] Sometimes he omits all formal setting, and breaks out at once into praise for his lady in honor of whom he is unable to refrain from song.

> Canteir m'estuet por la plux belle,
>   ke soit ou monde vivant,
>   car s'amor m'est tous dis novelle,
>   si en ai le cuor plux ioiant.[2]

The emotion of the poem, which is developed in a fairly conventional fashion, is uniformly that of a longing love. The first duty of the poet is to celebrate the charms of the beloved one. So he sings of her beauty and tells how

> cors ait bien fait et avenant,
>   euls vairs rians,
>   bouchete tainte en grainne.[3]

She is *dame sens peir, en la millor del roiame de France*,[4] a countess, a queen. Her beauty inspires his love and devotion at the same time that her dignified aloofness causes his grief. Indeed, his sorrow, usually barely mentioned in the beginning of the poem, in the end occupies nearly all his thought, as he closes with an appeal for mercy : —

> n'en ait mercit ne pities ne l'en prent,
>   morir m'estuet amerous en chantant.[5]

Because of the intimate relation which exists between this type of French secular lyric and several of the poems in this volume, it will be useful for the purposes of a closer comparison

---

[1] Bern MS. 389, No. CCLIII, *Archiv.*, 42.   [2] *Ibid.* No. LXXXVII.
[3] Bern MS. 389, No. XCI.   [4] *Ibid.* No. CCLXXIV.   [5] *Ibid.* No. CCL.

to give a characteristic specimen of this very popular kind of love poetry. One Gatier de Bregi sang thus of his love : —

Cant voi la flour et l'erbe vert pailie,
moi stuet chanteir por ma dolor covrir ;
car autrement ne puis avoir aïe
de celle riens cui i'ain tant et desire ;
s'en crien morir, tant redout lou faillir,
et losengiers, cui ie tant doi haïr,
quierent ma mort ne s'en puuent tenir.

En loiaulteit ai ma dame servie
come la riens cui tant ain et desir,
ne d'autre amor ne quier avoir amie.
Portant serai dou tout a son plaisir.
De mal sosfrir ne me doit sovenir,
car li grans biens ou ie cuis avenir
me fait mon cuer en ioie maintenir.

Jai fine amour ne me poroit retraire
k'envers ma dame aie nul ior fauceit,
ains l'amerai, car elle est debonaire.
En li ai mis cuer et cors et penseir.
Moult m'ont mi eul riche tressor moustreit, —
son tres gent cors sa bouche et sa biaulteit,
ke moult m'ait mort en mon bien destineit.

Ses simples vis rians et debonaires
et ses gens cors ou il ait tant biaulteit
m'ont si sospris ke ne m'en puis retraire,
n'en tout le (le) mont ne m'en vient plux engreit.
Tuit autre amant sont plux de moy greuei,
quant a ma dame cui ieu ain vient en greit.

Douce dame, prous et cortose et saige,
aies pitie de vostre amin chier !
Per maintes fois vos ai dit mon couraige.
Saichies de voir, loiaulment sens trichier,
vos amerai, c'autre desduit ne quier.
Se biauls servirs peust nul home aidier
bien me deüst ma dolour aligier.

Several of the Middle English religious lyrics have very obvious relations with the large class of French poems of which the above song is a fair specimen.

In general form many of the English poems are modeled directly after the French. No. 31, *An Orisoun to our Lady*, has in its meter and rhyme scheme been influenced by French lyrics. It has the typical five stanzas, and, like most of the French love songs of the class mentioned, has no refrain. No. 33 in form as well as in content suggests the *chanson*. The insertion of short lines and the arrangement of rhymes remind one of the French songs. No. 27 likewise takes the form of the French lyric. Finally No. 29 gives indications of a foreign connection in its length and in the tendency that it shows toward identical rhymes in its scheme, *aaaa abab*, and in the actual development of such rhymes in the third and fourth stanzas.

In this connection should be mentioned certain stylistic tricks that seem to have been imitated directly from the *chansons*. A favorite method of development with the *chansonniers*, and from them adopted by the English poets, was that of linking stanzas by converting the last verse of one stanza into the first of the next, sometimes transferring the line entire, sometimes taking only a prominent word or two, but retaining the thought. Many examples of its use can be found in these poems. In some cases, as in the poem whose first two stanzas are linked thus,

> leuedi, her mi bon.
>
> Mi bon þu her, leuedi der,[1]

it has been employed consistently and with good effect.

The abundant use of interjections, which is characteristic of the French songs, is also apparent in these poems. Expressions such as *Alas! welawei! pardee!* and many others, especially when used in songs that have other strong signs of

[1] No. 29.

French influence, suggest that medieval poets were often quite as much influenced by pernicious tricks of style as inspired by sheer poetic beauty. The French poet knew other ways of getting out of the difficulty presented by an empty half line, as is seen in the *chansons*, where conventional phrases, such as *jor et nuit*, become a welcome substitute for vacuity. When the first Middle English poets learned from their French neighbors the form and beauty of songs of love, they did not forget to learn also the secrets of the profession of love-singing. *Min hope is in þe, daჳ & nicht*, declares the English poet following closely the example found in France.

In content, however, the resemblance of the English religious lyric to its French models is even more marked than in matters of mere external form. The setting employed in several of the English poems has been taken directly from a French source, or has at least been influenced greatly by French songs. Thus Gatier de Bregi and a hundred others begin their lyrics with——

> Cant voi la flour et l'erbe vert pailie,

or similar nature settings, so the English poet sings,

> Nou skrinkeþ rose & lylie flour,
> Þat whilen ber þat swete savour,
> in somer, þat suete tyde ; [1]

and another French poet begins,

> De iolit cuer enamoreit
> chansonete comencerai,[2]

so the unknown English poet declares :

> Of þe, swete levedy, my song y wile byginne.[3]

But the influence of the French song writers extends far beyond mere settings, for in many cases it permeates the entire

---

[1] No. 33. [2] Bern MS. 389, CXXXIV, *Archiv*, 42–278.
[3] No. 65. MS. Harl. 2253.

D

emotion of the poem. The attitude of the English poet as he sings his love for Mary, who he remembers is now a 'peirles maide,' is not vastly different from that of the French writer who saw and celebrated charms more real to a worldly lover. Thus the English poet, unconsciously hoping to find in divine love a recompense for the deprivation which his religious devotion had cost him, easily substituted the Virgin for the '*douce dame*' of the secular French writer and as duly celebrated her excellencies.

No. 30 shows how intimately this spirit of the French secular songs had entered the English religious lyric. The poet's admiration for Mary's physical beauty is unbounded; he assures her that she is 'ful of þewes hende,' and in her graceful and courtly bearing she is a 'maide dreiȝ & wel itaucht;' in every charm, indeed, she is all-surpassing, for there is 'non swo swete of alle þing' nor

> nis non maide of þine heowe,
> swo fair, so sschene, so rudi, swo bricht.

Like the poet of worldly love, the English singer forgets not that his loved one has high rank, even royal, and he fittingly celebrates this distinguishing excellence : —

> þu ert icumen of heȝe kunne,
> of dauid þe riche king,
> nis non maiden under sunne
> þe mei beo þin euening.

Such high lineage, accompanied with all peerless charms, physical and moral, demands complete and constant devotion; so, like Gatier and all true lovers, while praying his lady for mercy, he vows that he is her faithful knight, ever at her service : —

> Ic crie þe merci : ic am þi mon,
> boþe to honde & to fote
> On alle wise þat ic kon.

The English poet, then, in uttering his cries for mercy has not prostrated himself before Mary of the liturgy, 'moost pitieous of alle pitieous wymmen'; nor is he altogether orthodox, one is forced to believe, for in his prayer he utters no irresistible plea for effective intermediation; he seems to have overlooked Mary's peculiar office. It is a return of affection for which he longs, while in his heart lie the pleading words of another nameless poet, 'Yif me þi love, ic am redi.' So the attitude of the lady of the French songs, always marked by dignity, aloofness, and a certain *hauteur*, is assumed by the English poet to be characteristic of Mary; and the constant appeal of the French lover,

> Douce dame, prous et cortose et saige,
> aies pitie de vostre amin cher,

finds its counterpart in the prayer of the English religious poet,

> Swete leudi, of me þu reowe
> & haue merci of þin knicht.

Likewise the poet of No. 64 evidently knew the spirit and conventions of the French song-writers. Aside from the shortness of the poem and other characteristics of form that point to a French influence, its emotional nature suggests that the ideas and experiences of worldly love as expressed in the *chansons* of France were known in England.

> Moder milde, flur of alle,
> þu ert leuedi swuþe treowe;
> bricht in bure & eke in halle,
> þi loue is euer iliche neowe.

The poet remembers the surpassing distinction of his lady, for she is a

> Riche quene and maiden bricht;

and he does not forget to plead for himself in the simple words,

> swete leuedi, of me þu reowe.

But the similarity of emotion between this poem and the *chansons* is not so close as in No. 30, for the poet apparently does not forget that it is Mary's protection in this world and her aid in the next that he most anxiously desires.

As pointed out previously, No. 31 had been influenced in its external form by the *chanson d'amour;* but in content, the poem does not afford many lines that prove a close relationship with French lyrics. The attitude of the poet toward Mary, although it is in many respects as orthodox as that of the liturgy, is not entirely so, for the spirit that pervades the poem as a whole is often suggestive of an earthly love. Like the French lover, the poet mentions in his first lines the subject of his song,

> On hire is al mi lif ilong,
> Of hwam ich wule singe;

and, though he has profited apparently by the sermon in the *Poema Morale,*[1] for he has a wholesome fear of sin and a consciousness of his own waywardness, he does not forget that Mary is the one 'þat is so freo,' and to her he cries, 'Leuedi, merci!'

Other songs in this volume show in a less uniform way traces of the influence of the general class of French lyrics that is richly represented in the Bern and Douce MSS.   Thus, Mary's charms are frequently insisted upon; like the earthly fair one, she has *un vis cleir;* she is the 'feirest flour of eni felde,' and 'a rose in eerbir so red'; her eyes are gray, and her body full of grace and courtly freedom.

> Ladi louelich, feir and fre,
> Þou lilye whyt of face,
> Godus Moder briht of ble,
> We tristen to þi grace.

---

[1] No. 31 has one line that is exactly paralleled in the *Poema Morale;* and there are other evidences of such influence.   Cf. the note on p. 17.

Since a lady possessing such charms must needs have a host of admiring friends, the French poet does not hesitate to mention this popularity. The same theme is even more aptly celebrated in regard to Mary. Many are the poets that rejoice in the honor that 'our lady' commands in the earth, for verily, 'þi worschipe walkeþ wyde.'

Such beauty, honor, and high birth demand vows of complete devotion and constant service. As the French lover offers himself to his lady and becomes her knight,[1] so the English religious poet, as instanced above, binds himself to the service of the Virgin and declares : —

> Serwte and serwise we owe, parde,
>   To thi hiȝnesse of very due,
> As royall most by pedigre,
>   None lyke of grace ne of vertu,
>   Lovely lady, þi servauntis trew.[2]

Before the *chanson d'amour* became in France the ruling form for the expression of subjective emotion, a peculiar kind of lyric poetry had flourished there, the *chanson à personnages*. These *chansons* are always narrative in form, with strangely combined lyric and dramatic tendencies. In the simplest and most typical form of this poem the writer tells as an introduction how the other day, *l'autrier*, wandering through a forest, by chance he overheard a woman complaining of her jealous husband; he then proceeds to give the words of the unfortunate wife. In later poems the laments are sometimes assigned to a maiden who complains of unrequited love; after this the next logical step is to report in other poems the

---

[1] There is an interesting manuscript described in the *Cat. de Manuscrits du Fond Français*, p. 316, which contains a collection of the Miracles of the Virgin. One of the rubrics tells 'D'un chevalier qui ne vouloit avoir aultre femme fors que la virge Marie.'

[2] No. 69. Such examples have sometimes been referred to by English critics as showing the influence of chivalry, and so they do, but undoubtly it is the influence of chivalry upon French poetry.

griefs of a lover.[1]   The essential characteristic, then, of this
class of poetry is that the poem is almost entirely a complaint,
usually of a woman, with an introduction in which the narrator
explains how he happened to hear about the sorrows which he
reports.

There is little variation in the introductions which these
poets allow themselves.   The following is typical : —

> L'autrier lonc un bosc fulhos
> > Trobiey en ma via
> Un pastre mout angoyssos,
> > Chanteir, e dizia
> > Sa chanson : . . . [2]

The *chanson à personnages* seems to have died out in France
a century before its influence was felt greatly in England, for
it was not until well into the fifteenth century that poems
imitated from this type became popular, when the religious
poets were evidently among the first to make extensive use of
it.   Often they put the words into the mouth of the Virgin,
lamenting the death of Christ.

A rather late poem, No. 5, shows how the *chanson à per-*
sonnages was easily adapted to religious uses.

> As I wandrede her bi weste,
> > ffaste vnder a forest syde,
> I seiȝ a wiht went him to reste,
> > Vnder a bouȝh he gon a-byde ;
> > Þus to crist ful ȝeor[n]e he criȝede,
> > And boþe his hondes he held on heiȝ :

Then follows the complaint of a penitent, who rehearses his
sins in detail.

---

[1] For other types of the *chanson à personnages*, see G. Paris, *Les Origines*, etc.
681 ff.

[2] Raynouard, II, 230.   The poem quoted from is, of course, the song of a
troubadour.

As mentioned above, the *chanson à personnages* assumed various forms. In one of these it is the lover himself that complains of unrequited love. The introduction in this class of poems, though of necessity somewhat changed from that of the earlier complaint form, was an adaptation of the *L'autrier* formula.

Two of the poems of Harleian MS. 2253 help to prove the assertion that the '*chanson à personnages* must have been taken over into English at the time when it flourished in France.'[1] One of these lyrics begins :—

> Þis enderday in o morewenyng,
> wiþ dreri herte ant gret mouryng
> on mi folie y þohte;
> one þat is so suete a þing
> þat ber iesse, þe heuene king,
> merci y besohte.[2]

The second poem is very similar in its setting : —

> from petres bourh in o morewenyng
> as y me wende omy pley yng,
> on me folie y þohte;
> menen y gon my mournyng
> To hire þat ber þe heuene kyng,
> Of merci hire bysohte.[3]

In a more general way the first stanza of No. 50 recalls the setting of many French secular poems, not necessarily *chansons*.

> In Somer bi-fore þe Ascenciun
> At Euensong on a Sonundai
> Dwellyng in my deuocioun
> ffor þe pees fast gon I prai :
> I herde a Reson to my pai,

---

[1] Padelford, *Early Sixteenth Lyrics*, p. xxxviii. The date of the Harleian MS. is the early fourteenth century.   [2] No. 27.   [3] No. 33.

Þat writen was with wordes þre,
And þus hit is, schortly to say:
Mane nobiscum domine.

The mention of the season, of the day with the time and atten-
dant circumstances, and of the answer 'writen with wordes
þre,' all indicate the ultimate influence of French poems,
though it would be rash to say that the lyric quoted owes
much directly to any French form.   This kind of introduction
became extremely popular in England in all classes of poetry;
it is probable that the above stanza owes more to English
than to French models.

The influence of the French religious lyric is neither easily
nor satisfactorily determinable.   The religious song in France
dates back almost as far as does the secular lyric itself.   Wace
relates that in the eleventh century the Virgin Mary appeared
before certain sailors, and saving them from a violent storm,
gave explicit directions for the founding of the *Feast of the
Conception at Caen*.   Considerably later, similar *fêtes* in honor
of the Virgin were established at Rouen, Dieppe, Arras, Valen-
ciennes, and other places, until by the fifteenth century there
had sprung up, all over France, societies that sought to honor
the Mother of God by contesting in song.   We do not know
at what time the composition of poems became the chief
characteristic of these *fêtes*.   In 1325 such a contest took
place, but it is almost certain that long before that date there
had been many hymns sung to the Virgin on these occasions.
However this may be, during the fourteenth and fifteenth
centuries there grew up in France a class of religious poetry
connected exclusively with these feasts.

The rules of different *puys*, as these partly literary, partly
religious, societies were called, varied somewhat; but in
general, so far as we can judge, the procedure followed fairly
uniform lines.   The *puys* usually lasted about ten days, each
day being given up to composing and reciting hymns, or

serventois, in honor of the Virgin. The poems were usually strained and artificial. The form of the *serventois* early became conventionalized. There were normally three stanzas of eleven lines each and an envoy of four or five lines, in which the presiding officer and judge, the 'Prince,' was addressed. There was also a refrain and other technical requirements into which it is not necessary to enter here.

Starting with these *serventois*, or at least greatly influenced by them, the practice of singing songs to Mary soon spread to all parts of France, and affected nearly all kinds of lyric poetry. The *serventois* became extended in its scope and seems to have included almost any song to the Virgin.[1]

Divine poems took also other forms and names; so we find Jean Molinet declaring: 'Autre couleur de rhethorique nommee simple lay est assez usite en oroisons, requestes et loenges.'[2] He then gives an example of a *lai* that is indeed sufficiently removed from the form of the *serventois*.

Out of the secular *chanson d'amour* there grew another class of religious lyrics, which was related neither to the formal *serventois* nor to the *lai;* it was rather an adaptation of the *chanson* itself for religious purposes. Thus in the Bern MS. we find several *chansons de nostre dame* that employ the same general form and the same phraseology as the secular lyrics in the same volume. Gautier de Coinci, also, used several *chansons d'amour* as models for his songs to Mary, in some cases employing even the rhymes that his predecessors had used. Not only were *chansons d'amour* turned to religious uses, but almost every other type of the secular lyric was made over to fit the exigencies of religious verse.[3]

---

[1] The term was also employed for a kind of satirical song, a use which of course does not concern us here.

[2] Langlois, *Recueil*, p. 241.

[3] On religious imitations in French poetry, see P. Meyer in Romania, XVII, 429–437; *ibid.*, Romania, XIX, 297–299; Jeanroy, Romania, XVIII, 477–486; Bulletin soc. anc. textes Fran. 1886, pp. 70 ff.; cf. also Novati, *Studii Critica*, pp. 179–310.

The influence that the French religious lyric, in its various forms and during its long development, exerted upon the poems in this volume seems to have been remarkably slight. The formal *serventois* with its set form and literary flavor was quite beyond the Middle English poet. Evidently it did not greatly appeal to his naïve taste. Still, there are hints that this kind of lyric, though unattempted in England, was not unknown there. No. 5, which in its introduction shows so clearly the influence of the *chanson à personnages*, indicates in other ways that its author was something of a literary artist and one who knew a little of foreign conventions, although he chose to throw all these marks of literary acquirement confusedly into one poem rather than to follow any one form consistently. The use of a refrain is doubtless French, and may well come from the *serventois*, in which, so far as I am aware, it was never lacking. It should be mentioned here, however, that the *serventois* is almost identical in form with many of the French *ballades*. Since the conventions of these two classes of poetry are largely the same, it is impossible to say which type the poet is trying to imitate. More striking than the use of a refrain, which may have come from any one of several sources, is the manner in which in the last stanza the poet, dropping the complaint form, substitutes his own words; thus in a way he secures a kind of envoy, which he carries out further by suddenly addressing Christ, calling Him the 'Prince of alle pite' just as the poet of the *puys* exclaimed in his *evoi*: —

> Prince d'amours, noble fu la maistrie,
> Quant sanz charnel meffait fist son cher filz,
> Amant parfait, homme en dame infinie
> Dont amans sont par grace resjoïs.[1]

Other poems in this collection have refrains that suggest a more or less intimate relation with French lyric poetry of the

[1] *Serventois couronné* in *Miracles de Nostre Dame*, Soc. des anc. textes Fran., 4, pt. iii, 237.

ballade type, but it may be safely said, as a result of actual comparison of the two, that the formal *serventois* found hardly an echo in the religious poetry of England. As for the *lais* that Molinet mentions, it is probable that they also were without influence, though it is somewhat hasty to speak definitely while so many French poems remain in manuscript.

Concerning the influence of the French religious imitation of the *chanson d'amour* it is even more difficult to decide. Like the English songs to Mary, these French parodies took over to their use external form, phraseology, and to some extent emotional qualities that had previously belonged to the secular lyric; but in doing this they differed from the English lyrics in several respects.

The French *chanson* poets, when they turned to writing religious verse, had had a long training in the art of writing. It seems to have been the usual procedure for a poet to devote himself in his youth to composing spirited secular poetry in which he spent his strength in celebrating the charms of a worldly love. It was not until he felt his powers waning, and fear seized upon his soul, that he turned to Mary, of whose efficacious aid he now stood in dire need, but of whose graces he was no longer in a mood to sing spontaneously and well. Consequently we are not surprised to find in these religious *chansons* a spirit of literary art, a feeling for convention, and an artificiality that is far removed not only from the simplicity of the English songs, but also from the superb emotional expression of the French secular lyrics. The French religious *chanson*, building upon a form that was already becoming worn out, lacks in general the outspoken enthusiasm that characterized the English poems.

It is not possible to prove conclusively that the religious imitation of the *chanson* exerted little influence in England. Still, it is evident that the impassioned songs of Gautier de Coinci, though often modeled after the secular *chanson d'amour*, did not affect English poetry, for his tricks of style, which are very marked, are not repeated in these lyrics. It is equally evident that the colorless religious song like the following, often found in the Bern MS. and elsewhere, was not widely sung in England : —

> De la meire Deu doit chanteir
> chascuns ki seit faire chanson
> k'anemins ne puet enchanteir.

Another fact that must be borne in mind is, that in France the religious *chanson* was not so popular as other forms of religious verse. Most of the religious poets preferred the conventional *serventois* as a form in which to express love for Mary.

It may be that now and then the English poet translated from some religious French poem, but on the whole the lyrics of this collection showing the influence of the *chanson* breathe a spirit of sincerity and a freedom from restraint and literary convention which forbid our thinking that they can be an imitation of an imitation, or indeed an imitation at all; for the English poet, working out his own bent, has in no case produced a thoroughly typical *chanson* either in form or spirit.

In the fourteenth century and before, there also flourished in France another kind of religious poetry. In style this was very ornate; it employed long words, and delighted especially in placing an adjective of many syllables in the rhyme; it abounded in allusions and in all kinds of ornaments and embellishments. A single line will illustrate admirably the nature of these lyrics : —

> O femme resplendissans, roïne glorieuse ! [1]

This literary affectation soon spread to England. Chaucer in translating his ABC poem from De Guileville's *Pélérinage de la vie humaine*, managed to preserve the spirit and manner of the original, thereby inaugurating a new school of English lyric

[1] Cat. Gén. des MS. des Bib. Publ., 17–22.

poetry. He was followed by Gower, Occleve, Lydgate, and some anonymous poets. The influence is felt in only one of these poems — the *Hymn to the Virgin*, No. 69, the thought and diction of which are sufficiently ornate to prove a connection with this class of poetry.

The influence of French upon the Middle English penitential lyric, then, comprises that derived, first, from the secular, and secondly, from the religious, lyric. The *chanson d'amour* exerted the greatest influence upon Middle English lyric verse. Many of the poems in this volume are modeled directly after the *chansons* in both form and content. The *chanson à personnages*, likewise, affected the English lyrics, particularly in their external form. The religious poetry of France, however, found hardly an echo in English lyric verse, for its conventional and highly literary character did not appeal to the unsophisticated poets of England.

MIDDLE ENGLISH PENITENTIAL LYRICS

A GENERAL CONFESSION

1. (A I a 1)   Brit. Mus. Royal MS. 17 B. XVII. fol. 4.

I know [to Go]d, ful of myght,
& [to his] modir mayden bright,
    & [to alle h]alouse here,
& [to þe, fa]dre gastly,
þat I [have s]ynned largely,   5
    In mony synnes sere:
In thoght, in speche, & in delite,
In worde, & werk I am to wite
    and worth to blame;
þer-fore I praie saynt mary   10
and alle halouse haly,
    In gods name,
and þo preste to praye for me,
þat god haue merci & pyte,
    for his manhede,   15
of my wreched synfulnes,
& gyue me grace & forgyuenes
    of my mys-dede.

A FORM OF CONFESSION

2. (A I a 2)   Vernon MS.

I was vn-kuynde,
And was þennne blynde,
    To worche aȝeynes his wille,

47

þat furst me wrouȝt,
And seþþe me bouȝt, 5
 Fro peynes he was put to ille;
þer-fore we pray
To þe to-day,
 þat knowes boþe good and ille,
Graunt vs lyue, 10
We may vs schriue,
 Vr penaunce to folfille.

GENERAL CONFESSION OF SINS

3. (A I b 1)   Rawlinson MS. B. 408.

I knowlech to god, with veray contricon,
 Vn-to seynt mary, and his seyntis alle,
Þat, þorgh my frealte and wrecchid condicion,
 In-to many synnes ofte haue I falle;
 But aftir mercy now wille I calle, 5
  With true confession, repentaunce,
  (God graunt me space), and due penaunce.

First: I knowlech þat I haue broken
 His x. commaundementis in many a place,
In werke, in worde, in þought, in token; 10
 And ofte be vnkynd vn-to his grace;
 Sweryng by his body, or by his face,
  Taken in ydul his blessid holy name:
  Wherfore y knowlech me gretely to blame.

I haue not loued hym and dred as I shuld, 15
 Neither serued hym in kepyng myne holyday;
But rather to playes & Iapes y wolde,
 Then to serue god, rede, syng, or pray.
 Al þe circumstaunce y can not say,

So synful y am and so vnstable,   20
For my defautes ben innumerable.

My fader and moder I haue not obeyed,
  As y shuld haue done, with helpe or mekenesse,
The balance of vertues I haue mysweyed,
  With sleyng of tonge, or with wilfulnesse,   25
  With lechory, or with þefte, or fals witnesse,
    Couetyng wykkydly man or mannes wyfe
    And oþer gode þat longed to þer lyfe.

The seuen dedely synnes I can not excuse:
  For I am gylty, in many maner wyse,   30
With delectacyon, consente, and vse;
  Al now to reherce I may not suffyse;
  In Pryde, Envye, wrath, Lechory, & couetyse,
    Sleuth, and Glotony, with al þer spices.
    Alas! al my life is ful of vices!   35

And my fyue wyttes I haue ofte myspend;
  To many vanytes castyng my syght,
And with my heeryng ful ofte y offend;
  My smellyng, my tastyng, I spend not ryght,
  My handes to synne haue ben ful light.   40
    Thus haue I gouerned my wittes fyve,
    And in synne mispended al my lyve.

The werkes of mercy I haue not fulfilled,
  Aftir my power, as ofte as I myght:
To helpe þe pore I was not beste willed,   45
  With mete and drynke and cloþing þem dyght,
  ȝeuyng no herborogh a-dayes or nyght,
    Helpyng no prisoners, ne vysyting þe seeke;
    To bery þe dede I was not meke.

E

The gostely werkes y haue lefte also :   50
    To councel and teche þem þat were lewde,
Geuyng no comfort in socour and wo,
    Neyther to chaste such as were shrewde,
    And so þer harmes not sore me rewed,
      Neyther forȝeuyng with true pacience,   55
      Or prayed for þem þat dide me offence.

I haue not reuerensed þe seuen sacramentes
    Þat ben ordenyd for my saluacion,
But of sore synned þat me repentes
    Aftir my baptym and confirmacion ;   60
    My orders or wedlok standith in accusacion.
      God graunt me penawnce, and holy brede,
      And holy anoyntyng, or I be dede.

Al þis I knowlech in general,
    Of synnes doyng, and leuyng good werkes.   65
ȝif I shulde nombre þe branches especial,
    I shulde occupy to wryte þer-of many clerkes.
With synful lyfe my sowle derkes
    That I can not see and lasse my defautes,
    And euer my enemyes maketh many sautes.   70

Now light me, holygost ! with þi presence ;
    And ȝeue grace my lyfe to amende,
With drede, and pyte, and trew science,
    With gostely strength to make a good ende.
    Thy gracyous councel to me now sende,   75
      With such vnderstondyng, and clere wisdome,
      That y may come to þi kyngdome.

A CONFESSIOUN TO IHESU CRIST

4. (A I b 2)   Vernon MS.
    Swete Ihesu crist, to þe
    A gulti wrecche Ich ȝelde me

ffor sunnes þat ichaue ido
In al my lyf hider-to.
In Pruide, in Envye, In lecherye,   5
In Sleuþe, In Wraþþe, in Glotenye,
In al þis worldus Couetyse,
Ichaue isunged In alle þyse.

I-broken Ichaue þi Comaundemens
Aȝeynes myn owne Conciens,   10
And not iserued þe to queme:
Lord Merci, ar þe dom is deme.

To ofte ichaue in my lyue
Isunged in my wittes fyue,
Wiþ Eres I-herd, wiþ Eiȝen siht,   15
Wiþ sunful speche day and niht,
Wiþ Honden I-hondlet, wiþ feet I-go,
Wiþ Neose i-smullet eft also,
Wiþ herte sunfulliche I-þouht,
Wiþ al my bodi vuel I-wrouht: 20
And of alle my folye
Merci, lord Ihesu, Ich crye.

Al-þauh ichaue i-sunged euere,
Lord, i ne forsok þe neuere,
Ne oþur god ne tok i none,   25
ffadur of heuene, but þe one.
And þerfore, lord, i þe biseche
Wiþ rihtful hertliche speche,
Ne ȝif þou me none mede
Aftur my sunfule dede.   30

But aftur, lord, þi grete pite
Ihesu lord, asoyle þou me,
And send me ofte, ar I dye,
Serwe in herte, and ter in eiȝe,
ffor sunnes þat ichaue i-do   35

In al my lyf hider-to.
And let me neuere eft biginne
To do no more dedly synne,
So þat I at myn endyng-day
Clene of synne dye may,   40
Wiþ Schrift and Hosul at myn ende ;
So þat my soule mowe wende
In to þat blisful Empyre
Þer þat þou regnest lord and sire.

Swete ladi seinte Marie,   45
fful of Alle Curtesie,
Modur of Merci and of pite,
Myn hope, myn help is al in þe.
Wel ich wot, ibore þou were
In help of al vs wrecches here ;   50
And wel ich wot þat alle þing
Þi sone wol don at þi biddyng.
Bi-sech þi sone lef and dere
ffor me synful wrecche here ;
Bi-seche him, for þe loue of þe   55
Þat he haue merci of me ;
And help me at myn ende-day
ffrom þe foule fendes affray.

Bi-seche also þe flour of alle,
Þi sone, for my frendes alle,   60
Þat he hem kepe wiþ his grace
ffrom alle perels in vche place,
And ȝef hem god lyf and god ende,
And Ioye whon þei schul heþene wende ;
And also alle cristene men.   65
God lord Ihesus, Amen, AMEN.

Seint Michel and seint Gabriel
And alle þe Angeles also wel :

Preyeþ for me to vre ladi,
Þat Ihesus of me haue merci.   70

Holi Patriarkes and prophetes,
Alle i preye ow and bi-seches:
Preyeþ for me to vre ladi,
Þat Ihesus of me haue merci.

Peter and Poul, þe Apostles alle,   75
Alle i beo-seche ou ȝerne and calle:
Preyeþ for me to vre ladi,
Þat Ihesus of me haue merci.

Seint Steuene and seint Laurens
And alle gode Martires þat þoleden turmens: 80
Preyeþ for me to vre ladi,
Þat Ihesus of me haue Merci.

Seint Martin and seint Nicholas
And alle gode confessours þat euer was:
Preyeþ for me to vre ladi,   85
Þat Ihesus of me haue merci.

Seinte Katerine and seinte Mergrete
And alle þe virgines gode and swete:
Preyeþ for me to vre ladi,
Þat Ihesus of me haue merci.   90

Seinte Marie Maudeleyne,
To þe I preȝe and eke pleyne:
Preyeþ for me to vre ladi,
Þat Ihesus of me haue merci.

Alle Halewen þat euere were,   95
Þat beoþ crist lef and dere:
Preyeþ for me to vre ladi,
Þat Ihesus of me haue merci.

AS I WANDREDE HER BI WESTE

5. (A II 1)   Vernon MS.

As I wandrede her bi weste,
  ffaste vnder a forest syde,
I seiȝ a wiht went him to reste,
  Vnder a bouȝh he gon a-byde;
Þus to crist ful ȝeor[n]e he criȝede,   5
    And boþe his hondes he held on heiȝ
  " Of pouert, plesaunce & eke of pruide,
    Ay, Merci, God, And graunt Merci.

God, þat I haue I-greuet þe
  In wille & werk, in word and dede,   10
Almihti lord, haue Merci of me,
  Þat for my sunnes þi blod gon schede!
Of wit & worschupe, weole & wede
  I þonke þe, lord, ful Inwardly;
Al in þis world, hou euere I spede,   15
    Ay, Merci, god, And graunt Merci.

Graunt Merci, god, of al þi ȝifte,
  Of wit & worschupe, weole & wo;
In to þe, lord, myn herte I lifte,
  Let neuer my dedes twynne vs a-two.   20
Merci þat I haue mis do,
  And sle me nouȝt sodeynly!
Þouȝ ffortune wolde be frend or fo,
    Ay, Merci, God, And graunt Merci.

I am vnkuynde, and þat I knowe,   25
  And þou hast kud me gret kuyndenes;
Þerfore wiþ humbel herte and lowe,
  Merci and for-ȝiuenes

Of Pruyde and of vnboxumnes!
  What eueri sonde be, þus sey I,   30
In hap and hele, and in seknes,
    Ay, Merci, god, And graunt Merci.

Graunt Merci, God, of al þi grace,
  Þat fourmed me wiþ wittes fyue,
Wiþ ffeet and hond, & eke of face   35
  And lyflode, whil I am alyue.
    Siþen þou hast ȝiue me grace to þryue,
      And I haue Ruled me Rechelesly,
    I weore to blame, and I wolde striue,
      But Merci, God, And Graunt Merci.   40

Merci þat I haue mis-spent
  Mi wittes fyue! þerfore I wepe;
To dedly synnes ofte haue I asent,
  Þi Comaundemens couþe I neuer kepe;
  To sle my soule In sunne I slepe,   45
    And lede my lyf in Lecheri,
  ffrom Couetyse couþe I neuere crepe;
    Ay, Merci, God, And Graunt Merci.

Of oþes grete and Gloteny,
  Of wanhope and of wikked wille: 50
Bacbyte my neiȝhebors for enuy,
  And for his good I wolde him culle;
  Trewe men to Robbe and spille,
    Of Symony and with surquidri;
  Of all þat euere I haue don ille,   55
    Ay Merci, God, And graunt Merci.

Bi lawe I scholde no lengor liue
  Þen I hedde don a dedly synne;
Graunt Merci þat ȝe wolde forgiue,
  And ȝeue me space to mende me Inne!   60

ffrom wikked dedes & I wolde twynne,
   To Receyue me ȝe beo redi
In-to þi blisse þat neuer schal blynne,
   Nou Merci, God, And graunt Merci.

Graunt Merci, for þou madest me,   65
   Merci, for I haue don a-Mis;
Min hope, Min help is hol in þe,
   And þou hast ȝore bi-heiht me þis:
   Whos euere is Baptiȝed schal haue Blis,
     And he Rule him Rihtwysli.   70
   To worche þi wille, lord, þou me wis!
   Nou Merci, God, And graunt Merci.

Soþfast god, what schal I say,
   how schulde I amendes make,
Þat plesed þe neuere in-to þis day   75
   Ne schop me nouȝt mi sunnes forsake?
   But schrift of mouþe mi sunnus schal slake
     And I schal sece and beo sori,
   And to þi Merci I me take.
   Nou Merci, God, [And] Graunt Merci."   80

ffader & sone and holigost,
   Graunt Merci, God wiþ herte liht,
ffor þou woldest not þat I weore lost.
   Þe ffader haþ ȝiuen me a miht,
   Þe sone a science and a siht   85
     And wit to welde me worschupely,
   Þe Holigost vr grace haþ diht.
   Nou Merci, God, And graunt Merci."

Þis is þe Trone þat twynned neuere,
   And preued is persones þre,   90
þat is and was and schal ben euere,
   Only God in Trinite;

help vs, Prince of alle pite,
  Atte day þat we schal dy,
Þi swete face þat we may se.   95
    Nou Merci, God, And Graunt Merci.

I WITE MY SELF MYNE OWNE WOO

6. (A II 2)   Rawl MS. C. 86..

fol. 71   In my youth fulle wylde I was,
          My self þat tyme I cowde not knowe,
          I had my wylle in euery place,
          And þat hath browȝt me now so lowe.
          To chastice me þu didist it I trowe!   5
          Thynke, Jhesu, I am þyne owne!
          ffor me were þy sydes bloo;
          I wite my self myne owne woo!

          I made compromite trewe to be,
          ffirste whanne I baptisid was;   10
          I toke þe worlde and went fro þe,
          I folowd þe fende in his trace;
          ffrom envie wold I not pas;
          With couetise I was cauȝt also,
          My flessh had his wille, [alas!]   15
          I wite my self myne owne woo!

          lorde, I had no drede of þe;
          Thy grace went Away þerfor;
          But, lorde, siþen þu bouȝtist me,
          Thow woldest not þat I were lore.   20
fol. 71ᵇ   ffor me þu sufferste peynes sore;
          Thow my frende and I þy foo;
          Mercy, lorde, I wolle no more;
          I wyte my self myne owne woo!

Now I wote I was full*e* wylde,   25
ffor my will*e* passid my witte;
I was full sturdy and þu full*e* mylde,
lorde, now I knowe well*e* hit.
Off þy blisse I were full*e* qwyte,
Yf I had yt after þat I haue do;   30
But to þy me*r*cy I truste yt;
I wite my self myne owne woo!

hygh of herte I was and prowde,
And of cloþyng wondir gaye;
I loked þ*at* men shuld to me lowte   35
Were þ*at* I wente in þe waye.
On women and on good araye,
All my delite stode only þerto;
Ayen þy techyng I said naye;
I wyte my self myn*e* owne woo!   40

All*e* my truste was on my goode,
More þan on god þ*at* me hit sent;
Welth made me high of mode;
luste and lykynge me ou*er* wente.
To gete good I wolde not stynte;   45
I ne rawghte how þat I came þerto;
fol. 72 To þe pore neþ*er* gave ne lente;
Therfore I wite myselfe myn*e* owne woo.

Ther be þre poyntes of myschef
That arn confusion to many A man,   50
Whych þ*at* makyth þe saule greve;
I shall hem tell*e* as I can:
Pore men prowde þat litell*e* han,
That wolde be arrayed as ryche men goon;
Yf þey do folye, and be taen   55
They may wite hem self her owne woo!

A ryche man A thef is A noþer,
That of covetise wolle not slake.
Yf be wrong [he] be gyle his broþer,
In blisse he shalle be forsake.   60
Byfore god thefte is take;
Alle þat with wrong he wynneth so;
But yf þat he A mendis make,
he shalle wite him self his owne woo!

Olde man lechour is þe þirdde;   65
ffor of complexcioun waxeth colde.
hit bryngeth þe soule payne Amydde;
hit stynketh on god many folde.
Thyes pre þat I haue of tolde
Arn plesyng to þe fende, owre foo.   70
hem to vse who is so bolde
May wite hym self his owne woo!

fol. 72^b   Man take hede what þu art!
But wormys mete þu wote wel þis!
Whanne þe erthe hath take his parte,   75
heven or helle wolle haue his.
Yf þu doest welle þu goest to blis;
Yf þu do eville vnto þy foo;
love þy lorde, and thynke on þis,
Or wite þy self þyn owne woo!   80
                        ffinis

A PRAYER TO OUR LADY

7. (A II 3)   Add. MS. 27,909.

Leuedi sainte marie, moder and meide,
þu wisie me nuþe for ich eom eirede;
vnnut lif to longe ich lede,
hwanne ich me biþenche, wel sore ich me a-drede.

Ich eom i-bunde sore mid wel feole seonne,
mid smale and mid grete, mid wel feole cunne.
dai and nicht ich fundie to wendende heonne
wielde Godd an heuene to hwucchere wunne.

Slep me haŏ mi lif forstole richt half oŏer more;
awai to late ich was iwar; nu hit me reoweŏ sore   10
inne slepe ne wende ich endie nocht, þech ich slepe euremore.
hwao se lifeŏ þat wakerur beo þencþ of mine sore.

Al to longe slepŏ þe mann þat neure nele awakie.
hwo se understant wel his ende-dai, wel ȝeorne he mot spakie
to donde sunne awei fram him and fele almesse makie;   15
ȝif him ne schal hwanne he forŏ want, his brei gurdel quakie.

Slep me haŏ mi lif forstole er ich me bisehe;
þat ich wel aȝitte nu bi suhŏe of min ehe.
mi brune her is hwit bicume, ich not for hwucche leihe;
and mi tohte rude iturnd al in-to oŏre dehe.   20

Ifurn ich habbe isunehed mid worke and mid worde,
hwile in mine bedde and hwile atte borde.
ofte win idrunke and selde of þe forde.
muchel ich habbe ispened; to lite ich habbe an horde.

Hord þat ich telle, is almesse-dede: 25
ȝieue þe hungrie mete and te nakede iwede,
rede þe redliese þat is wiŏ-ute rede,
luuie god almichti, and of him habbe drede.

Ifurn ich habbe isuneȝet mid wurken and midd muŏe;
and mid alle mine lime siŏŏe ich sunehȝ cuŏe.   30
and wel feole sunne ido þe me ofþincheŏ nuŏe,
and swo me hadde ifurn ido, ȝif hit me crist i-ȝuŏe.

Moder, ful of milce, ibidde mi mod wende;
laete me steowi mi flesc, and mine fo schiende;

edmodnesse luuie to mine lifes ende;   35
luue to gode and te mann, ic bidde þat tu me sende.

Leuedi sainte marie, understond nu seonne mine.
ber min erende wel to deore sune þine,
hwas fle[s]ch and blod ihalȝed is of bred, of water, of wine,
þat us ischulde he eure fram alle helle pine.   40

Inne mete and inne drinke ic habbe ibeo ouerdede,
and inne wel sittende schon in pruttere iwede.
hwanne ich ihurde of gode speke, ne hedd ich hwat me sede.
hwan ich hier-of rekeni schal, wel sore me mei drede.

HEȝE LOUERD, ÞOU HERE MY BONE

8. (A II–4)   Harl. MS. 2253.

Heȝe louerd, þou here my bone,
þat madest middelert & mone,
   ant mon of murþes munne;
trusti kyng, ant trewe in trone,
þat þou be wiþ me sahte sone,   5
   asoyle me of sunne.
ffol ich wes in folies fayn,
In luthere lastes y am layn,
   þat makeþ myn þryftes þunne;
þat semly sawes wes woned to seyn,   10
Nou is marred al my meyn,
   away is al my wunne.

   vnwunne haueþ myn wonges wet,
   þat makeþ me rouþes rede;
Ne semy nout þer y am set,   15
þer me calleþ me fule flet,
   ant waynoun! wayteglede.

whil ich wes in wille & wolde,
In vch abour among þe bolde
  yholde wiþ þe heste;   20
Nou y may no fynger folde,
Lutel loued, ant lasse ytolde,
  y leued wiþ þe leste.
A goute me haþ ygreyþed so,
ant oþer eueles monye mo,   25
  ynot whet bote is beste;
þat er wes wilde ase þe ro,
nou yswyke, y mei nout so,
  hit siweþ me so faste.

ffaste y wes on horse heh,   30
  ant werede worly wede;
Nou is faren al my feh,
wiþ serewe þat ich hit euer seh,
  a staf ys nou my stede.

when y se steden styþe in stalle,   35
ant y go haltinde in þe halle,
  Myn huerte gynneþ to helde;
þat er wes wildest in wiþ walle,
nou is vnder fote yfalle,
  ant mey no fynger felde.   40
þer ich wes luef, icham ful loht,
ant alle myn godes me at goht,
  myn gomenes waxeþ gelde;
þat feyre founden mi mete & cloht,
hue wrieþ awey, as hue were wroht,   45
  such is euel ant elde.

Euel, ant elde, ant oþer wo
  foleweþ me so faste,
me þunkeþ myn herte brekeþ a tuo;
suete god, whi shal hit swo?   50
  hou mai hit lengore laste?

whil mi lif wes luþer & lees,
glotonie mi glemon wes,
　　wiþ me he wonede a while;
prude wes my plawe fere,　　　　　　　　55
lecherie my lauendere,
　　wiþ hem is gabbe & gyle.
Coueytise myn keyes bere,
Niþe ant onde were mi fere,
　　þat bueþ folkes fyle.　　　　　　　　60
Lyare wes mi latymer,
sleuthe & slep mi bedyner
　　þat wheneþ me vnbe while.

vmbe while y am to whene,
　　when y shal murþes meten;　　　　　　65
monne mest y am to mene:
lord, þat hast mi lyf to lene,
　　such lotes lef me leten!

such lyf ich haue lad fol ȝore;
merci, louerd! y nul namore,　　　　　　70
　　bowen ichulle to bete;
syker hit siweþ me ful sore;
gabbes les & luþere lore
　　Sunnes bueþ vn sete.
godes heste ne huld y noht,　　　　　　75
bote euer aȝeyn is wille ywroht,
　　mon lereþ me to lete.
such serewe haþ myn sides þurhsoht,
þat al y weolewe a way to noht,
　　when y shal murþes mete.　　　　　　80

To mete murþes ich wes wel fous,
　　ant comely mon to calle;
ysugge by oþer ase by ous:
alse ys hirmon halt in hous,
　　ase heueþ hount in halle.　　　　　　85

Dredful deþ, why wolt þou dare
bryng þis body, þat is so bare,
   ant yn bale ybounde?
Careful mon ycast in care,
yfalewe as flour ylet forþfare,   90
   ychabbe myn deþes wounde.
murþes helpeþ me no more;
help me, lord, er þen ich hore,
   ant stunt my lyf a stounde!
þat ȝokkyn haþ yȝyrned ȝore,   95
Nou hit sereweþ him ful sore,
   ant bringeþ him to grounde.

to grounde hit haueþ him ybroht:
   whet ys þe beste bote?
bote heryen him þat haht vs boht,   100
vre lord, þat al þis world haþ wroht,
   ant fallen him to fote.

Nou icham to deþe ydyht,
   ydon is al my dede;
god vs lene of ys lyht,   105
þat we of sontes habben syht,
   ant heuene to mede!
     amen.

GOD, ÞAT AL ÞIS MYHTES MAY

9. (A II-5)   Harl. MS. 2253, fol. 106, a.

God, þat al þis myhtes may,
   in heuene & erþe þy wille ys oo,
ichabbe be losed mony a day,
   er ant late y be þy foo;

Ich wes to wyte & wiste my lay;   5
   longe habbe holde me þer fro;
vol of merci þou art ay,
   al vngreyþe icham to þe to go.

To go to him þat haþ ous boht,
   my gode deden bueþ fol smalle;   10
of þe werkes þat ich ha wroht
   þe beste is bittrore þen þe galle.
My god ich wiste, y nolde hit noht,
   in folie me wes luef to falle;
when y my self haue þourh soht,   15
   y knowe me for þe worst of alle.

God, þat deȝedest on þe rod,
   al þis world to forþren & fylle:
for ous þou sheddest þi suete blod,
   þat y ha don, me lykeþ ylle;   20
bote er aȝeyn þe stiþ ystod,
   er & late, loude ant stille,
of myne deden fynde y non god;
   lord, of me þou do þy wylle.

In herte ne myhte y neuer bowe,   25
   ne to my kunde louerd drawe;
my meste vo ys my loues trowe,
   crist ne stod me neuer hawe.
Ich holde me vilore þen a gyw,
   & y my self wolde bue knawe!   30
Lord, merci, rewe me now!
   reyse vp þat ys falle lawe!

God, þat al þis world shal hede,
   þe gode myht þou hast in wolde;
on erþe þou come for oure nede,   35
   for ous sunful were boht & solde;

F

when we bueþ dempned after vr dede
 a domesday, when ryhtes bueþ tolde,
when we shule suen þy wounde blede,
 to speke þenne we bueþ vnbolde.   40

vnbold icham to bidde þe bote,
 swyþe vnreken ys my rees;
þy wey ne welk y ner afote,
 to wickede werkes y me chees;
fals y wes in crop ant rote,   45
 when y seyde þy lore wes lees;
Iesu crist, þou be mi bote,
 so boun icham to make my pees.

Al vnreken ys my ro,
 louerd crist, whet shal y say?   50
Of myne deden fynde y non fro,
 ne noþyng þat y þenke may.
vnworþ icham to come þe to,
 y serue þe nouþer nyht ne day;
In þy merci y me do,   55
 god, þat al þis myhtes may.

THE PRAYER

10. (B a I a 1)   Horae MS. in York Minster Library.

lorde iesu cryste, leuand god sone,
Þu set þi deyd, þi cros, and þi passione,
Be-twix þi dome, & my saul, for deyd þat I haue don,
Now [and] at my endyng þat I be noght fordon.
And graunte us mercy, & grace whyls we er on lyue,   5
Un-to þi kyrke, un-to þi rewme, for þi wondys fiue;
forgyuenes & reste to þaim þat to ded ere dryue,
joy to al synful: þis graunt us be-liue.
þu þat liues, þu þat reynnes, god wit-owtyn ende
in werld of werles wit ioy þat euer sal lende.   10

LOVERD, SHYLD ME VROM HELLE DETH

11. (B *a* I *a* 2)   Porkington MS. No. 10.

Loverd, shyld me vrom helle deth at thylke gryslich stounde,
When hevene and oerthe shulle quake and al that ys on grounde,
When thou shalt demen al wyth fur, that ys on oerthe
    y-vounde.
             Libera me, Domine, etc.

Ich am overgard agast, and quake al in my speche,   5
Aȝa the day of rykenyng and thylke gryslych wreche,
When hevene and oerthe shulle quake, and al that ys on grounde.
That day ys day of wreythe, of wo, and soroufolnesse;
That day shall boe the grete day, and voul of bytternesse,
When thow shalt demen al wyth fur that ys on oerthe
    y-vounde.   10
Thylke reste that ever last, loverd, thow hoem sende,
And lyht of hoevene blysse hoem shyne wythouten ende!
Crist, shyld me vrom deth endeles, etc.
What, ich vol of wrechenesse, hou shal ich take opon,
When ich no god ne bringe to-vore the domes mon?   15

IN MANUS TUAS

12. (B *a* I *a* 3)   Arundel MS., 292.

     Loverd Godd, in hondes tine
     I biqueðe soule mine,
     ðu me boctest wið ði deadd,
     Loverd Godd of soðfastheedd.

TO OUR LADY

13. (B *a* I *a* 4)   York *Horae* MS.

    Blessyd marye, virgin of nazareth,
      And moder to the myghty lorde of grace,

That his people saued hath with his deth
  From the paynes of the infernall place;
  Now blessyd lady, knele before his face,   5
And praye to hym my soule to saue from losse,
Whiche with his blode hath bought us on the crosse.

PREY WE TO THE TRINYTE

14. (B *a* I b 1)   MS. Engl. Poet. e. I.

    Prey we to the Trinyte,
    And to al the holy compane,
    For to bryng us to the blys,
    The wych shal never mysse.

Jhesus, for thi holy name,   5
  And for thi beter passyon,
Save us frome syn and shame
  And endeles damnacyon;
And bryng us to that blysse,
That nevere shal mysse.   10

O gloryusse lady, quen off heven,
  O mayden and o mothere bryght,
To thy sonne with myld steven
  Be owr gyde both day and nyght;
That we may cum to that blysse,   15
The wych never shal mysse.

Gabryell and Raphaell,
  With scherapyn and seraphyn,
Archangell Mychaell,
  With all the orderes nyne,   20
Bryng us to that blysse,
The wych never shal mysse.

O ye holy patryarkys,
  Abraham, Ysaak, and many moo,
Ye were full blyssed in yowr werkes,   25
  With Johan the Baptyst also,

For to bryng us to that blysse,
The wych never shal mysse.

The holy apostoles off Cryst,
   Petur, Paule, and Bartylmewe,   30
With Thomas, and Johan the evangelyst,
   And Andrew, Jamys, and Mathewe,
Bryng us to that hevenly blysse,
The wych never shall mysse.

Pray fore us ye seyntys bryght,   35
   Stevyn, Laurence, and Cristofore,
And swete Georg, that noble knyght,
   With all the marters in the qwere,
That we may cum to that blysse,
The wych never shall mysse.   40

Blyssyd confessor, sent Gregory,
   With Nycholas, and Edward kyng,
Sent Leonard, and Antony,
   To yow we pray above all thyng,
To helpe us to that blysse,   45
The wych never shal mysse.

O yow blyssed matrones,
   Anne and swet sent Elsabeth,
With al the gloryus vyrgyns,
   Kateryne and noble sent Margaret,   50
Bryng us to the hevenly blysse,
The wych never shal mysse.

All the company celestyall,
   The wych do syng so musycall,
To the kyng pryncypall   55
   Pray fore us terrestyall,
That we may cum to that blysse,
The wych never shall mysse.

A SHORT PRAYER AFTER THE LEVATION
FOR MERCY

15. (B a I c 1)   Brit. Mus. Royal MS. 17 B. XVII.

Lord, als þou con, & als þou wille,
haue merci of me, þat has don ille;
for what-so þou with me wil do,
I holde me payde to stonde þer-to;
þi merci, ihesu, wold I haue,   5
and I for ferdnes durst hit craue,
bot þou bids aske, & we shal haue;
swete ihesu, make me saue,
And gyue me witt & wisdame right,
to loue þe, lord, with al my might.   10

A PREYER AT ÞE LEUACIOUN

16. (B a I c 2)   Vernon MS.

I þe honoure wiþ al my miht
In fourme of Bred as i þe se,
Lord, þat in þat ladi briht,
In Marie Mon bi-come for me.

Þi fflesch, þi blod is swete of siht,   5
Þi Sacrament honoured to be,
Of Bred and Wyn wiþ word i-diht;
Almihti lord, I leeue in þe.

I am sunful, as þou wel wost:
Ihesu, þou haue merci of me;   10
Soffre þou neuere þat I be lost
ffor whom þou diȝedest vppon þe tre,
Ac þorwh þat ladi of Merci most
Mi soule þou bringe in blisse to þe;

Repentaunce to-fore mi deþ,   15
Schrif[t] and Hosul þou graunte me,
Wiþ ffadur and Sone and Holygost,
Þat Regneþ God In Trinite.   Amen.

IHESU, FILI DEI, MISERERE ME

17. (B a I c 3)   Add. MS. 5665.

Ihesu, fili dei, miserere me !
Glorius god in trinite,
well of man and pyte,
thus cryed the woman of canany :
  miserere mei, miserere mei !   5

Thou came fro heuen fro thi se
To this worlde a man to be ;
Ther for y crye deuoteli,
  Miserere mei !

As þou haddest vn hir pyte,   10
So y pray thou haue vn me
Glorius god in trinite,
  Miserere mei !

PRAYER FOR GOD'S MERCY

18. (B a I c 4)   Rawlinson MS. B 408.

Now, god almyghty, haue mercy on me,
  For maryes prayers and al þi sayntes,
To whom, wepyng and knelyng on kne,
  Thus now I make my complayntes.
    For sorow and shame my hert ful fayntes ;   5
      Wherfor of al my synnes mercy I cry,
      And pray the to bryng to heuen an hy.

PRAYER TO MARY

19. (B a I c 5) Rawlinson MS. B 408.

I pray þe, lady, þe moder of crist,
Praieth ȝoure sone me for to spare,
With al angels, and Iohn Baptist,
And al ȝoure company þat now ys thare.
Al holichurch, for my welfare, 5
Graunt me of ȝoure merites a participacion,
And praieth oure lorde for my saluacyon.

PRAYER TO ST. ELENE

20. (B a I c 6) MS. in York Minster Library.

Seint elene, j þe pray
To helpe me at my last day
To sette þe crosse and his passione
Betwix my synfull saule and dome;
Now, and in þe houre of my dede, 5
And bring my saule to requied.

DEUS IN NOMINE TUO SALUUM ME FAC

21. (B a I c 7) Cotton Calig. A. ii.

fol. 64^b God in thy name make me safe and sounde,
And in thi vertu me deme & justifie;
And as my leche sarch vn to the grounde
That in my soule ys seke, and rectifie;
To haue medicine afore thi dome y crye, 5
Wherfore of endeles mercy ay & grace,
That y desposed be vch day to dye,
And so to mende whylle y haue tyme & space.

God, graciously here thou my prayere,
The wordes of my mouth with ere perceyue;   10
And as thou on the rode hast bought me dere,
To make me able thi mercy to receyue,
Yf that the fende with frawde wolde me deceyue,
In thi ryght syde ther be my restyng place,
Wher ys my comfort, as y clere conceyue,   15
Whych may me mende whille y haue tyme & space.

For alienes, lord, haue ryse a gaynes me,
And peple stronge my sely soule haue sought;
But for they purpose not to loke on the,
Gramarcy, lord, hir malyce greueth nought.   20
Thi passioun be emprinted in my thought,
The chefe resort my fleschly foo to chase;
On hit to be remembred welle y aught,
Which may me mende whylle y haue tyme & space.

Be hold for soth, þat god hath holpen me,   25
And of my soule our lord ys vp taker.
Wher y was thralle, lord, thou hast made me fre.
Whom shalle y thank bot the, my god, my maker?
When y shalle slepe, my keper and my waker,
In eueri perylle, my confort and my grace,   30
For of the synfulle art thou not forsaker,
That wylle amende whille they haue tyme & space.

Turne euell thynges vnto my mortalle fon,
And in thi treuth dispytt hem and spylle,
So that they be confounded euerychone,   35
That wolde me stere to dysobaye thi wylle.
The dewe of loue and drede on me distylle,
Thatt dedely synne ne do me not deface,
fol. 65   That y thi hestys fayle not to fulfylle,
Whech may me mende whylle y haue tyme & space.40

I shalle do to the wylfulle sacrifice,
And knoulech to thi name, for it is good;
Alle oder worldely weele y wylle dispice,
That floweth oft and ebbeth as the floode.
Thy blessed body, sacred flesh and blode,   45
With alle my hert beseche y euer of grace,
Hit to receyue in clennes for my foode;
hit may me mende whille y haue tyme & space.

For fro alle trouble thou hast delyuered me,
And on enmyes myne eye hath had despite;   50
Wher fore y Wylle perseuer alle day with the,
In fulle entent that kyndenesse for to quite,
And, that y may performe thus my delite,
Salve me, Lorde of mercye and full of grace,
That neuer the fende me finde oder plite,   55
But euer to mende whille y haue tyme & space.

Joye to the fader, fulle of grace & might,
Whos hye powere alle thyngis may preserue;
Joye to the sone, that in a [holy] virgyn lyght,
And for oure gylt vpon a cros wold sterue;   60
Joye to the holy gost that doth conserue
Oure clere conceyte by confort of his grace;
A blessed trinite welle owe we to reserue,
Luynge to the whille we haue tyme & space.

That ys and was with owte begynnyng,   65
Thre in oo substaunce, hye god in commbtable,
With owte ende eternalle enduryng,
Alle myghty, ryghtwys and mercyable;
Gracious to alle contrite and confortable;
Both lord and leche to alle lust haue grace,   70
Wyth oyle of mercy to mescheue medcynable,
Hele alle hut of synne with tyme and space.
                        Explicit.

IHESU, MERCY FOR MY MYSDEDE!

A deuoyt Meditacione

22. (B a II a 1)   Trin. Coll. Cambridge, B. 10, 12.

Ihesu, mercy! mercy, I cry:
 myn vgly synnes þou me forgyfe.
þe werlde, my flesch, þe fende, felly
 þai me besale both strange & styfe;
I hafe ful oft to þaim consent,   5
 & so to do it is gret drede;
I ask mercy with gud entent;
 Ihesu, mercy for my mysdede!

þe werlde thurgh his fals couetyse,
 þe fende with pryde, wreth, ire, envy, 10
I hafe, ihesu, bene fylde oft sythys,
 my flesche with slewth & lychery,
And oþere many ful gret synnes;
 with repentance, ihesu, me fede,
for euere my tyme opon me rynnes: 15
 Ihesu, mercy for my myse-dede!

Turne not þi face, ihesu, fro me,
 þof I be werst in my lyfynge;
I ask mekely mercy of þe,
 for þi mercy passes al thynge.   20
In þi fyue woundes þou sett my hert,
 þat for mankynde on rode walde blede,
& for þi dede vgly & smert,
 Ihesu, mercy for [my] myse-dede!

To þi lyknes þou has me made;   25
 þe for to lufe þou gyfe me grace;
þou art þe lufe þat neuere sal fade;
 mercy I ask whils I hafe space.

I tryst ihesu of forgyfnes
  of al my synnes, þat is my crede;   30
I me betake to þi gudnes;
  ihesu, mercy for my myse dede!

Als touchande grace, bot ask & hafe:
  þus has þou het in þi beheste,
þar for sum grace on þe I crafe;   35
  with outen grace I am bot beste,
& warre þan beste defyled with syne;
  þou graunt þat grace may in me brede,
þat y þi lufe, ihesu, myȝt wynn:
  Ihesu, mercy for my myse dede!   40

Al worldely lufe is vanite;
  bot lufe of þe passes al thynge.
þar is no lufe with outen þe;
  & þe to lufe I aske syghynge.
Ihesu, me graunt lufe þe forthy,   45
  & in þi law, ihesu, me lede.
þat I myslufede, I aske mercy:
  Ihesu, mercy for my mysdede!

It is of þe for to forgyfe
  alkyn tryspas both more & mynn;   50
It is of me, whyls I here lyfe,
  or more or lesse ilke day to synne,
And of þe fende to duell þer in:
  þou gyfe me grace to take gud hede
þat I þi lufe, ihesu, myght wynne!   55
  Ihesu, mercy for my myse dede!

Dispyce me noȝt, swete lorde ihesu,
  I am þe warke of þin aghen hende,
þof I hafe bene to þe vntrew;
  Ihesu, þou kan me sone amende;   60

þou has me made to þi lyknes,
 thurgh synne I hafe loste heuenly mede;
Now, lorde, I aske of þi gudenes,
 Ihesu, mercy for my myse dede!

þow walde be borne for synful man,   65
 for syn þou take no wreke on me.
My comforth be þi harde passione;
 Ihesu, þer of hafe I gret nede;
For synne þou graunt me contrycione:
 Ihesu, mercy for mysdede!   70

After my dedes þou deme me noȝt;
 after mercy þou do to me;
If þou me deme als I hafe wroght,
 in bytter payns I drede to be.
My lyfe to mende, & hafe mercy,   75
 My lorde ihesu, þou be my spede,
luf þe, & drede, þat syttis on hy:
 Ihesu, mercy for my myse dede!

If I had done ilke cursed warke,
 & alken synnes wer wroȝt in me,   80
þou may þaim sleke, als is a sparke
 when it is put in myddes þe see;
& þar may no man sleke my myse
 bot þou, ihesu, of þi godhede;
when þou wouchesafe, þou sone forgyfese: 85
 Ihesu, mercy for my mysdede!

Who sal þe loue in fynyal blyse
 bot trow mankynde & angels fre?
Myne heretage forsoth þat is:
 thurgh gude lyfeynge & grace of þe,   90

þou me restore vnto þat blyse;
  beholde frelete of my manhede
þat makes me oft to do of myse:
  Ihesu, mercy for my myse dede!

Þo[u] wil no dede of synful man: 95
  þus says þou, lorde, in haly wryt;
Ful wele wote þou coueytis þan
  he turne his lyfe & sone mende it:
þou gyfe me grace my lyfe to mende,
  beswylede in synn als wyckede wede;   100
graunt me þi lufe with outen ende:
  Ihesu, mercy for my myse dede!

Þow art my god, I þe honour;
  þou art þe sone of maydyn & moder,
In my dysese þou me succure,   105
  þou art my lorde, þou art my brother;
þou sal me deme, my cryatour,
  when vp sal ryse euere ilke a lede.
Mercy, ihesu, my sauyour!
  Ihesu, mercy for my myse dede!   110

Þou helpe me, lorde, in my dysese,
  þat walde susan helpe in hir tyme;
Ful gret clamour þan gon þou pese
  when scho acusede was of crime.
þou sett my saule, myn hert, in ese,   115
  þe fende to flee & his falshede,
& soferandely þe for to plese:
  Ihesu, mercy for my mysedede!

In my baptym I mayde beheste
  þe for to serue lelely & wele;   120
Of þi seruyse oft hafe I seste,
  with synnes thowsandes serued vnsele;

Bot þi mercy nedes moste be sene
  þer moste synn is & wyckededede;
þe moste synful I am, I wene;   125
  Ihesu, mercy for my myse dede!

For synful man walde þou be borne;
  for ryghtwys not þou wil recorde;
when man had synnede, he was forlorne,
  & þan him kyndely þou restorde;   130
þou sufferde paynes coronde with thorne,
  nakede with outen clath or schrede,
with mykel sorue þi body torne:
  Ihesu, mercy for my mysedede!

Þou art my hope, my way ful sure,   135
  ay lastande hele, both streng[t]h & pese;
þou art pyte þat ay sal dure;
  þou art gudenes þat neuer sal sese;
þou art clennes, both mylde & mure;
  me þe displese, ihesu, for bede,   140
Als þou was borne of virgyne pure:
  ihesu, mercy for my myse dede!

Þou byddes ilke man ȝelde gud for ille,
  not il for il to ȝelde agayne;
þan I beseke þe þat þou wil   145
  graunt me mercy in stede of payne!
þou me forgyfe, & mercy graunt,
  & in my saule þou sawe þi sede,
þat I may, lorde, make myne auaunt:
  Ihesu, mercy for my myse dede!   150

Bot, worthy lorde, to þe I cry,
  & I in syne stande obstynate;
þarfore þou heres noȝt me forthy,
  þou will noȝt here me in þat state.

þou gyfe me grace lefe my foly,   155
   & fe[r]uently þe lufe & drede,
þan wate I wele I get mercy :
   Ihesu, mercy for my myse dede!

Noght euere-ilke man þat cales þe lorde,
   or mercy askes, sal hafe þi blise,   160
his consciencȝ bot he remorde,
   & wirke þi wil, & mende his lyfe.
To blyse sal I sone be restorede,
   if I my saule þusgates wil fede ;
Of þi mercy late me recorde :   165
   ihesu, mercy for my mysedede!

I me betake to þi mercy
   þat mercy gyffes to synful men ;
þou kepe me, lorde, for I sal dye,
   & wot neuere whore, ne how, ne when.   170
In þi hote lufe me graunt to brene,
   & þat lesson trewly to rede ;
Mercy þou graunt! amen! amen!
   Ihesu, mercy for my myse dede!   Amen.

AN ORISOUN TO VR LORD IHESU

23. (B a II a 2)   Vernon MS.

Lord, Swete Ihesu crist : Haue Merci of me,
Þat out of heuene come : In to eorþe for me,
And of þe Mayden Marie : Boren were for me,
And on þe cros suffredest : Bitter deþ for me.

Of Merci I þe bi-seche : Þat mest of mihtes may,   5
Swete Ihesu my cumfort : Mi solas and my play ;
Of alle vices me deliuere : And of pruide, I þe pray,
Þat I may þe louen as lord : And knowen for God verray.

fful muchel ouhte i þe to louen : In stable treuþe and fay,
Whon þou were god & art : And schalt ben euere and ay, 10
Com in to eorþe for my loue : To take my kuynde of clay,
In þe world to wynne vs wele : Þou suffredest men worchen þe
    way.

In þe werld, as I seide er : In bodi, fflesch and Bon,
Hunger and ffurst heddestou boþe : In hot and Cold to gon,
Blod and watur þou swattest boþe : And Teres Mony on, 15
And seþþhen for þe loue of vs : Þi deþ þen hastou tan.

fful hard and deolful was þi deþ : Hose hedde hit in þouht,
Whon þat þi blessede bodi : Þat neuere no sunne wrouht,
Among þis false Iewes : Þi-seluen hast hit brouht,
And seþþen wiþ þi blessed blod : ffrom bale þou hast us bouht. 20

A Croune of þornes vppon þin hed : Þei setten scharp and
    fresch,
Heo þe nayleden hondes and feet : Boþe þorwh bon and flesch ;
A spere þorwh þi syde stong : Þyn herte was ful nesch,
Whon þe blod and watur sprong : Þat vs of synne wesch.

Þerfore, Ihesu, I preye þe : Þat ful art of pite, 25
ffor my sunnes þat ichaue don : Let me neuere dampned be ;
But graunte me grace in to myn herte : Ihesu in Trinite,
Of stable treuþe and rihtwys werkes : Loue and Charite.

fful ofte ichaue þe wraþþed : And broke þi Comaundement,
Wiþ al my fyue wittes : In lyf þat þou me hast lent, 30
Vnwisliche hem dispendet : And not in good entent,
Boþe þorwh myn owne wille : And oþure entisement.

Bote, swete Ihesu, woltou me here : wiþ schrift ichaue þe
    souht ;
In mony werkes, as I seide ere : Vuele ichaue I-wrouht,
    G

Non of hem schal ben vnpunissched—: Þeron is al my þouht; 35
I take me al to þi Merci: ffor loue for-ȝet me nouht.

Wiþ Mylde mod and sikyng sore: I be-seche þe
ffor my ffrendes, Ihesu crist: As well as for me.
On domes-dai whon þou schalt demen: Scheuh us þi face freo,
And bring vs in to paradys: Þer endeles blisse schal beo.   Amen.

IHESU CRISTE, HAUE MERCY ONE ME

24. (B a II a 3)   Thornton MS.

    Ihesu Criste, haue mercy one me,
    Als þou erte kynge of mageste,
    And forgiffe me my synnes all
    þat I hafe donne bathe grete and small,
    And brynge me, if it be thi will,   5
    Till heuene to wonne ay with þe styll.   Amen.

HER BIGINNEÞ AN ORISUN OF ÞE TRINITE

25. (B a II a 4)   Vernon MS.

    Fadur and Sone and Holigost,
    Lord, to þe I crie and calle,
    Studefast god of mihtes most,
    My sunful lyf is steken in stalle:
    I preye þe, lord, þat þou þe haste,   5
    Me to helpe, þat I ne falle,
    And mak my soule clene and chaste
    Of dedly sunnes and vueles alle.

    Lord, haue Merci of my synne,
    And bring me out of al my care;   10
    Euele to do wol I nou blynne.
    I haue I-wrouht aȝeynes þi lawe:

Þou rewe of me [boþe] out and Inne,
And hele me of my woundes sare;
Lord, þat al þis world schal winne,   15
Hele me ar i fonde and fare.

Fadur in heuene þat wel may,
I preye þe, lord, þat þou me lede
In rihte weyes of stable fay;
At myn endynge whon I haue drede,   20
Þi grace ich aske [boþe] niht and day,
And ȝif me merci of my misdede.
Of myn askyng sei not nay,
But help me, lord, at al my nede.

Swete Ihesu, for me was boren,   25
Þou here my preyere loud and stille,
ffor pyne þat me is leid bi-foren
Ofte i sike and wepe my fille.
Ofte so haue I ben for-sworen
Whon I haue don aȝeynes þi wille,   30
Suffre neuere þat I beo loren,
Lord, for myne dedes ille.

Þe holygost, i preye to þe
Niht and day in good entent,
Of al my serwe cumforte me,   35
Þin holi grace þou me sent,
And schild me, ȝif þi wille be,
ffrom dedly sunne, þat I ne beo schent,
ffor Marie loue, þat Maiden fre,
In whom þou lihtest, verreyment.   40

I preye þe, ladi Meoke and mylde,
Þat þou preye for my misdede,
ffor [þe] loue of þi swete childe,
As þou him sauh on Rode blede.

Euerȝite haue I ben wylde,   45
Mi sunfol soule is euere in drede:
Merci, ladi, þou me schilde,
And helpe me euere at al myn nede.

Merci, Marie, Mayden clene!
Þou let me neuere In sunne dwelle,   50
Preye for me þat hit beo sene,
And schild me from þe pyne of helle.
ffor certes, ladi, riht wel i wene
Þat al my fomen maiȝt þou felle.
ffor-þi my serwe to þe I mene,   55
Wiþ ferful mod my tale i telle.

Bi-þenk þe, ladi, euere and ay
Of alle wimmen þou berest þe flour:
ffor sunfol mon, as I þe say,
God haþ don þe gret honour.   60
Receyue my preyere niht and day,
Whon I þe be-seche in eny a Our;
Help me, ladi, so wel þou may,
Me bi-houeþ þou beo my counseilour.

Off counseil, ladi, i preye to þe   65
Niht and day, in wele and wo;
Of al my serwe cumforte me,
And beo my scheld aȝeynes my fo.
ffor, certes, ȝif þi wille hit be,
Al my fo-men maiȝt þou slo.   70
Help me, ladi hende and fre,
Þou take þat þe is fallen fro.

At myn endynge þou stonde bi me
Whon I schal henne fonden and fare,
Whon þat I quake and dredful be,   75
And al my sunnus I rewe hem sare.

As euere myn hope haþ ben in þe,
Þenk þeron, ladi, and help me þare,
ffor [þe] loue of þat swete tre
Þat Ihesu spradde [on] his bodi bare.   80

Ihesu, for þat ille stounde
Þat þou woldest on Rode blede,
At myn endynge whon I schal founde
Þou haue merci of my misdede,
And hele me of my dedlich wounde,   85
And help me in þat muchele nede;
Whon deþ me takeþ and bringeþ me to grounde,
Þen schal i, lord, þi domes drede.

Lord, for my sunnes to do penaunce,
ffor my dedes þou graunte hit me   90
A space of verrey Repentaunce
In serwe of herte, I preye to þe.
In þi merci is myn affyaunce;
Of my folye þou haue pite,
Þat þou of me ne take veniaunce,   95
Lord, for þi benignite.

Lord, as þow art ful of miht,
And as þou alle þinges wost
My lyf amende, my dedes riht,
ffor mari loue þat maiden chost,   100
And bringe me sone in to þat liht
Wiþ-outen ende þer ioye is most,
On þe to seo þat swete siht,
ffadur and Sone and Holigost.   AMEN.

DO MERCY TO FORE THI JUGEMENT

26. (B a II a 5)   Harl. MS. 1704.
fol. 26^b There is no creature but one,
          Maker of Alle creaturs,

One god And euer one,
iii in one all*e* waye endures.
To thatt lord we make oure mone   5
In whom is all*e* comfort And cure;
To thenk howe freel we be eu*er*ychone!
This world is but hard Aventure!
For who so most ys in assure
Sonnest is slayne And shent.   10
Whan thou this world w*ith* fyre shalt pure,
do mercy to fore thy jugement.

We aske mercy or thou deme,
lest thou dampne þ*at* þou hast wrought.
What joy were it the devill*e* to queme   15
to yef hym thatt þu hast bought?
fol. 27   And of thy sight thou vs flome,
We are but lost right as nought.
Nowe make us like such as we seme,
In loue And drede thou sett our þought.   20
ffor synne hath us so þorowgh sought
There is no trust in oure entent;
Yn to Acounte or we be brought,
do m*er*cy tofore thy jugement.

We aske mercy of rightnesnesse,   25
ffor þy behest*es* all*e* be right;
And of thyn owne kyndnesse
Saue yt þ*at* þu hast yeue vs of thy might.
This world is but likerous bitt*er*nesse
That reueth vs discrescion And sight;   30
The fende, the flesch*e*, fyght Ayen vs:
Thus we be take in turment.
Lorde, or thy dome be dight to vs
do mercy to fore thy jugement.

Thou hast bede vs aske And haue ;   35
That yeuyth vs comfort for to call*e* ;
and thou hast ordeygned man*e* to saue,
mercy A boue thy workes all*e*.
Also thyn hert blood thou for vs gaf,
make vs fre þat erst were thrall*e*.   40
let neu*er* the deuell*e* with sorow depraue
That wasch*en* was in holy well*e*.
Oure flesch*e* is freel that makyth vs fall*e* ;
With grace we rise And shull*e* repent,
And thus we hope þat we haue shalle   45
Mercy A fore thy jugement.

We aske mercy of all thyng,
and thou Art kynde in eu*er*y degre :
þou yaf vs with stonys beyng,

fol. 27^b   And with thy sprite endued vs f[ree] ;   50
With trees thou yaf vs growing,
With bestis felyng lyf haue we,
With Aungell*es* vnderstondyng,
With byleue wedded vn to the,
And with thy blode bought we be ;   55
Yet be we fals And necligent
That we mowe neu*er* clymuie ne fle
Thy mercy in thy jugement.

Wherefore oure soulis And our*e* lyff
in to thyn handys we betake   60
Oute of temptacou*n* And stryf
To saue vs when we slepe or wake.
Now Jh*es*u, for thy woundys v,
And also for thy moder sake,
The deuyl Away fro vs thou dryue   65
When deth shall his maistres make.

Thou saidest thou woldest not vs forsake,
When thou on the rood were rent.
Ayen thy dome we crie And quake,
Do mercy to fore thy jugement.   70

And yef thou deme vs rightnesly,
yiff mercy the execusion;
Alle though we haue seruyd þe vnkyndely,
Take hede to oure entencoun.
We yelde vs synfulle And sory   75
With knowlich And contricoun;
Oure bapteme And thy mercy
We take to oure proteccion.
Byleue is oure saluacoun
By lawe of thy Commaundement.   80
Now, crist, put alle thy passion
Be twyye vs And thy jugement.
　　　　　　Amen.

IESU CRIST, HEOUENE KYNG

27. (B a II a 6)   Harl. MS. 2253, fol. 75, b.

Iesu crist, heouene kyng,
ʒef vs alle god endyng,
　　þat bone biddeþ þe;
at þe biginnyng of mi song;
iesu, y þe preye among,   5
　　In stude aiwher y be;
ffor þou art kyng of alle,
to þe y clepie ant calle,
　　þou haue merci of me!

þis enderday in o morewenyng,   10
wiþ dreri herte ant gret mournyng

.on mi folie y þohte;
one þat is so suete a þing,
þat ber iesse, þe heuene kyng,
   merci y besohte.   15

iesu, for þi muchele myht
þou graunte vs alle heuene lyht,
   þat vs so duere bohtes;
for þi merci, iesu suete,
þin hondy werk nult þou lete,   20
   þat þou wel ȝerne sohtes.

Wel ichot, ant soþ hit ys,
þat in þis world nys no blys,
   bote care, serewe, & pyne;
þare fore ich rede, we wurchen so,   25
þat we mowe come to
   þe ioye wiþ oute fyne.

TO THE, MAIST PEIRLAS PRINCE OF PECE

28. (B α II a 7)   Gray MS., Advocates' Library, fol. 77–79.

To the, maist peirlas prince of pece,
With all my power I the pray,
Let neuir thi micht be merciles
Til man that thou has maid of clay.
Oure kynd is brukle, that is no nay,   5
And euir has bene sen thou maid ws;
Thairfore we nedis baith nycht and day
Of *miserere mei, Deus*.

We that ar heir baith fair and fresch
Sall fallou and faid / as dois a flour,   10
And all delitis of mannis flesch
Sall failye in less / than half ane hour;

Baith kyng and knicht and conquerour.
Dreid of fra this blis mon bus
And be fulfane to seke succour   15
At *miserere mei, Deus.*

Quhen we ar deid, and dollin deip,
And grene gress growis abone our brawn,
Quhat helpis than to wawill or weip?
Til this lif cum we neuir agane,   20
Bot also smal as droppis of rane
Wan wormys so schill sall all to schow ws,
And thak it is to lait to sayn,
Lord, *miserere mei, Deus.*

Quhy lufe we than that ilk life   25
That so litill quhile will lest,
Sen fathir and mothir, brothir and wife
And kyn and barnis / that we luf best,
Fra deid haff drawin ws till his nest.
Thai ar full fane to fle fra ws?   30
And than we think moist treuthfull trest
To *miserere mei, Deus.*

Heirfore me think suld dredand be
Man and woman and euery wicht;
It is na dowt / we mon all dee   35
For ilk wy a deid is dicht.
Quhat furtheris it with him to fecht
Sen fra him / is nane that chowus,
Prince no paip, my treuth I plicht,
But *miserere mei, Deus?*   40

Than helpis it nocht with him to strife
Aganis our dede / that we may dreid
That lichtly may sone downe drif
This wrechit warld of lynth and breid.

Ther is no money na no meid   45
With him may hauld a day of trewus,
Bot gif we faynd to speke and speid
With *miserere mei, Deus.*

For mercy maid our makir hevin;
Mary consawit throw gabriell stevin;   50
The suthfast god deit on rude,
With spere and nalis he bled his blude,
The gretast grace / that euir yet grew ws;
Therfor me think moist faithfull fude
Is *miserere mei, Deus.*   55

Now crist, that confortis all mankynd,
Thou lat thi pece spred and spring.
Oute of this warld, quhen we sall wend
Sa that na feynd to pane ws bring,
Bot haif in mynd this foresaid thing;   60
Jhesu nazareth, king of jewis,
And heir ws quhen we reid or syng
Of *miserere mei, Deus.*
                    Explicit.

HAIL, MARY!

29. (B *a* II b 1)   Digby MS. 2, leaf 6.

Hayl, mari! hic am sori:
haf pite of me, and merci!
mi leuedi, to þe i cri:
for mi sinnis, dred ham hi,
wen hi þenke hat hi sal bi,   5
  þat hi haf mis hi-don
in worde, in worke, in þoith, foli:
leuedi, her mi bon!

Mi bon þu her, leuedi der,
þat hic aske wit reuful cher!   10
þu len me her, wil hic am fer,
do penanx in mi praier;
ne let me noth ler, þat þu ber,
  at mi nendin day;
þe worlais, þai wil be her,   15
  fort[to] take þair pray.

To take þar pray, alse hi her say
þai er redi, boyt nite and day;
so strange er þai, þat we ne may
A-gaynis þaim stond, so way la way,   20
but þu gif helpus, mitteful may,
  Wit þi sunes grace;
Wan þu comes, þai flet a-wai;
  dar þai not se þi face.

þi face to se, þu grant hit me,   25
lefdi ful-fillid of pite,
þat hi may be in Ioy wit þe,
to se þi sone in trinite,
þat sufferid pine, and ded for me
  and for al man-kyn: 30
his flesse was sprade on rode tre,
  to leysus al of sine.

Of sine and kar, he maked vs bar,
Wan he þollid pines sar;
to drupe and dar, we athe wel mare,   35
alse for þe hondis doyt þe har,
wan we þenke hu we sal far
  wan he sal dem vs alle,
we sal haf ned[e þan &] þare,
  a-pon mari to calle, &c.   40

HYMN TO THE VIRGIN

30. (B a II b 2)   MS. 54, D. 5. 14, in Corpus Christi College, Oxford.

Edi beo þu, heuene quene,
folkes froure & engles blis,
moder unwemmed & maiden clene
swich in world non oþer nis.
On þe hit is wel eþ sene,   5
Of alle wimmen þu hauest þet pris.
mi swete leuedi, her mi bene,
& reu of me, ȝif þi wille is.

Þu asteȝe so þe daiȝ rewe;
þe deleð from [daiȝ] þe deorke nicht.   10
of the sprong a leome newe
þat al þis world haueð iliȝt.
nis non maide of þine heowe,
swo fair, so sschene, so rudi, swo bricht.
swete leuedi, of me þu reowe,   15
& haue merci of þin knicht.

Spronge blostme of one rote,
þe holi gost þe reste upon,
þet wes for monkunnes bote,
& heore soule to alesen for on.   20
Leuedi milde, softe & swote,
Ic crie þe merci; ic am þi mon,
boþe to honde & to fote,
On alle wise þat ic kon.

Þu ert eorþe to gode sede,   25
on þe liȝte þe heouene deuȝ;
of þe sprong þeo edi blede,
þe holi gost hire on þe seuȝ.

þu bring us ut of kare, of drede
þat Eue bitterliche us breuȝ;   30
þu sschalt us in to heouene lede.
welle swete is þe ilke deuȝ!

Moder, ful of þewes hende,
Maide dreiȝ & wel itaucht,
ic em in þine loue bende,   35
& to þe is al mi draucht.
þu me sschild ȝe from þe feonde,
ase þu ert freo, & wilt, & maucht.
help me to mi liues ende,
& make me wið þin sone isauȝt.   40

Þu ert icumen of heȝe kunne,
of dauid þe riche king;
nis non maiden under sunne
þe mei beo þin eueni[n]g.
ne þat swo derne louiȝe kunne,   45
ne non swo swete of alle þing.
þu bring us in to eche wunne,
i-hered ibeo þu swete þing!

Swetelic ure louerd hit diȝte
þat þu maide wið-ute were,   50
þat al þis world bicluppe ne miȝte
þu sscholdest of þin boseme bere.
þe ne stiȝte, ne þe ne priȝte,
in side, in lende, ne elles where;
þat wes wið ful muchel riȝte,   55
for þu bere þine helere.

þo godes sune aliȝte wolde
on eorþe al for ure sake,
herre teȝen he him nolde
þene þat maide to beon his make.   60

betere ne miȝte he, þaiȝ he wolde,
ne swetture þing on eorþe take.
leuedi, bring us to þine bolde,
& sschild us from helle wrake. AMEN.

AN ORISON OF OUR LADY

31. (B a II b 3)   Cotton MS. Caligula A ix, leaf 246.

On hire is al mi lif ilong,
Of hwam ich wule singe,
And herien hire þer-among,
Heo gon us bote bringe
Of helle pine þat is strong,   5
Heo brohte us blisse þat is long
Al þurh hire chilðinge.
Ich bidde hire one mi song,
Heo ȝeoue us god endinge,
Þah we don wrong.   10

Þu art hele and lif and liht,
And helpest al mon-kunne.
Þu us hauest ful wel idiȝt,
Þu ȝeue us weole and wunne;
Þu brohtest dai, and eve niȝt;   15
Heo broȝte woht, þu broȝtest riȝt;
Þu almesse and heo sunne.
Bi-sih to me, lauedi briȝt,
Hwenne ich schal wende heonne,
So wel þu miht.   20

Al þis world schal ago
Wið seorhe and wið sore,
And al þis lif we schule for-go,
Ne of-þunche hit us so sore.

Þis world nis butent ure ifo,   25
Þar-fore ich þenche hirne at-go,
And do bi godes lore.
Þis liues blisse nis wurð a slo;
Ich bidde god þin ore,
Nu and euere-mo.   30

To longe ich habbe sot i-beo,
Wel sore ich me adrede.
Iluued ich habbe gomen and gleo,
And prude and feire wede.
Al þat is dweole wel i seo,   35
Þar-fore ich þenche sunne fleo,
And alle mine sot dede.
Ich bidde hire to me bi-seo,
And helpe me and rede,
Þat is so freo.   40

Agult ich habbe, weilawei!
Sunful ich am an wrecche.
Awrec þe nu on me, leuedi,
Er deþ me honne fecche.
Do nim þe wreche, ich am redi;   45
Oþer let me liuen and amendi,
Þat no feond me ne drecche.
For mine sunnes ich am sori;
Of þis world ich ne recche.
Leuedi, merci! Amen.   50

A SONG TO THE VIRGIN

32. (B α II b 4)   Egerton MS. 613.

Of on þat is so fayr and briȝt,
  velud maris stella,
Briȝter þan þe day-is liȝt,
  parens et puella.

Ic crie to þe, þou se to me.   5
Leuedy, preye þi sone for me,
   tam pia,
Þat ic mote come to þe,
   maria

Of kare conseil þou ert best,   10
   felix fecundata.
Of alle wery þou ert rest,
   mater honorata.
Bi-sek him wiz milde mod,
Þat for ous alle sad is blod   15
   in cruce,
Þat we moten komen til him
   In luce.

Al þis world was for-lore,
   eua peccatrice,   20
Tyl our lord was y-bore.
   de te genitrice.
With aue it went a-way,
Þuster nyth and comet þe day
   salutis;   25
Þe welle springet hut of þe
   uirtutis.

Leuedi, flour of alle þing,
   rosa sine spina, ·
Þu bere ihesu heuene king,   30
   gratia diuina.
Of alle þu berst þe pris,
Leuedi, quene of parays,
   electa,
Mayde milde, Moder   35
   es effecta.

H

Wel he wot he is þi sone,
uentre quem portasti.
He wyl nout werne þe þi bone,
paruum quem lactasti.   40
So hende and so god he his;
He hauet brout ous to blis
  superni,
Þat hauez hi-dut þe foule put
  inferni.   45
Explicit cantus iste.

NOU SKRINKEÞ ROSE & LYLIE FLOUR

33. (B *a* II b 5)   Harl. MS. 2253, fol. 80, a.

Nou skrinkeþ rose & lylie flour,
þat whilen ber þat suete sauour,
  in somer, þat suete tyde;
ne is no quene so stark ne stour,
ne no leuedy so bryht in bour,   5
  þat ded ne shal by glyde.
whose wol fleyshlust forgon,
  & heuene blis abyde,
on iesu be is þoht anon,
  þat þerled was ys side.   10

from petres bourh in o morewenyng
as y me wende omy pleyȝyng,
  on mi folie y þohte;
menen y gon my mournyng
to hire þat ber þe heuene kyng,   15
  of merci hire bysohte:
Ledy, preye þi sone for ous,
  þat vs duere bohte,
ant shild vs from þe loþe hous
  þat to þe fend is wrohte.   20

myn herte of dedes wes for dred
of synne þat y haue my fleish fed,
   ant folewed al my tyme ;
þat y not whider i shal be led,
when y lygge on deþes bed,   25
   In ioie ore in to pyne.
on a ledy myn hope is,
   moder and virgyne ;
we shulen in to heuene blis
   þurh hire medicine.   30

betere is hire medycyn,
þen eny mede or eny wyn ;
   hire erbes smulleþ suete ;
from catenas in to dyuelyn
nis þer no leche so fyn,   35
   oure serewes to bete ;
mon þat feleþ eni sor,
   & his folie wol lete,
wiþ oute gold oþer eny tresor,
   he mai be sound ant sete.   40

of penaunce is hir plastre al,
ant euer seruen hire y shal
   nou & al my lyue ;
nou is fre þat er wes þral,
al þourh þat leuedy gent & smal ;   45
   heried be hyr ioies fyue !
wher so eny sek ys,
   þider hye blyue ;
þurh hire beoþ ybroht to blis
   bo maiden ant wyue.   50

for he þat dude is body on tre
of oure sunnes haue piete,
   þat weldes heouene boures !
wymmon wiþ þi iolyfte,

þou þench on godes shoures;   55
þah þou be whyt & bryht on ble,
    falewen shule þy floures.
Iesu, haue merci of vs,
    þat al þis world honoures.
            Amen.   60

THE BEST SONG AS HIT SEMETH ME

34. (B a II c 1)   Add. MS. 5665.

The best song as hit semeth me
peccantem me cotidie.

While y was yong and hadde carage
I wolde play with grome and page,
But now y am ffalle in to age   5
Timor mortis conturbat me.

Yowthe ys now ffro me agon,
and age ys come me vpon.
Now shall y say and pray anon,
    parce michi, domine.   10

I pray god y can no more;
þou bozsteste me with wondes sore;
To thy mercy thow me restore,
    saluum me fac, domine.

EVERE MORE, WHERE SO EUER I BE

35. (B a II c 2)   Bodl. MS. Engl. Poet. e. 1.

Evere more, where so euer I be
The dred of deth do troble me.

As I went me fore to solase,
I hard a mane sygh[e] & sey : alase,
Off me now thus stond the case,   5
    ye dred of [deth do trobyll me !]

I haue be lorde of towr & towne,
I sett not be my grett renowne,
ffor deth wyll pluck [yt] all downe!
   ye dred off deth do trobyll me!   10

Whan I shal deye I ame not suere,
In what countre or in what howere,
Where fore I sobbyng sey to my power:
   ye dred off deth do troble me!

Whan my sowle & my body departyd shallbe,   15
Of my Jugment, no man cane tell me!
Nor of my place wher yat I shal be:
   yerfore dred of deth do troble me!

Jhesu cryst whan yat he shuld sofer hys passyon,
To hys fader he seyd with gret deuocyon,   20
Thys is ye causse of my intercessyon:
   ye dred off deth do troble me!

Al crysten pepull, be ye wysse & ware,
Thys world is butt a chery ffare,
Replett with sorow & fulfyllyd with care!   25
   yerfore ye dred of deth do troble me!

Wheyer yat I be mery or good wyne drynk,
Whan yat I do on my last daye thynk,
It mak my sowle & body to schrynke,
   ffore ye dred of deth sore troble me!   30

Jhesu vs graunt hyme so to honowr,
That at owr end he may be owr socowr,
And kepe vs fro ye fendes powr,
   ffor yan dred off deth shal not troble me!

IN WHAT ESTATE SO EUER I BE

36. (B a II c 3)   Bodl. MS. Engl. Poet. e. i.

In what estate so euer I be
Timor mortis conturbat me.

As I went in a mery mornyng,
I hard a byrd boye wep & syng,
Thys was ye tenowr of her talkyng: 5
      timor, &c.

I asked yat byrd what sche ment,
I am a musket boye fayer & gent,
for dred of deth I am al schent:
      timor, &c.   10

Whan I schal dey I know no day,
what countre or place I can not sey,
wherfor yis song syng I may:
      timor, &c.

Jhesu cryst whane he schuld dey,   15
to hys fader he gan sey:
fader, he sayd, in trinyte,
      timor, &c.

All crysten pepull behold & se,
yis world is but a vanyte,   20
& replet with necessyte,
      timor, [&c.]

Wak I or sclep, ete or drynke,
whan I on my last end do thynk,
for grete fer my sowle do shrynke,   25
      timor, &c.

God graunte vs grace hym for to serue,
& be at owr end whan we sterue,
& frome ye fynd he vs preserue !
timor, &c. 30

ALAS, MY HART WILL BREK IN THRE

37. (B a II c 4)   Balliol MS. 354.

Alas, my hart wil brek in thre }
Terribilis mors conturbat me. } fote

Illa iuventus that is so nyse
me deduxit in to vayn Devise,
Infirmus sum, I may not Rise. 5
terribilis mors conturbat me.

Dum iuv[enis] ffui lytill I dred,
Se[d] semper in sinni[s] I ete my bred,
Iam ductus sum in to my bed,
terribilis mors [conturbat me]. 10

Corpus migrat in my sowle,
Respicit demon in his Rowle,
Desiderat ipse to haue his tolle,
terribilis mors [conturbat me].

Christus se ipsum, whan he shuld dye, 15
Patri suo his manhode did Crye:
Respice me, pater, that is so hye,
terribilis mors [conturbat me].

Quaeso Iam, the trynyte
Duc me from this vanyte, 20
In Celum ther is Joy with the !
terribilis mors conturbat me.
Explicit.

TIMOR MORTIS CONTURBAT ME

38. (B a II c 5)   Harl. MS. 2255.

fol. 128^b So as I lay this othir nyght
              In my bed, tournyng vp so don,
              Whan *phebus* with his beemys bryght
              Entryd the signe of the *lyon*,
              I gan remembre with Inne my reson   5
              Vpon wourldly mutabilite,
              And to recoorde wel this lesson:
              Timor mortis conturbat me.

fol. 129   I thoughte pleynly in my devise,
              And gan considre in myn entent,   10
              how *Adam* whyloom in paradise
              Desceyved was of a fals serpent
              to breke goddys comandement,
              Wheer thorugh al his posteryte
              lernyd by short avisement: 15
              Tymor mortis conturbat me.

              ffor styng of an *appyl* smal
              he was exyled froom that place;
              Sathan maade hym to haue a fall*e*,
              To lese his fortune and grace;   20
              And froom that gardeyn hym enchace
              ffulle ferre froom his felicite,
              And thanne this song gan hym manace:
              Timor mortis conturbat me.

              And had nought been his greet offence,   25
              And this greet transgression;
              And also, his inobedience
              Of malice and of presu*m*pcion;

Gyf credence agayn al reson
To the Develys iniquite;　　　　　　　　　　30
We had knowe no condicion
Of *timor mortis conturbat me.*

This lastyd forth al the age;
ther was noon othir remedye;
The venym myght nevir a swage　　　　　35
Whoos poyson sprong out of envye,
Off pryde, veynglorye, and surquedye;
And lastyng til tyme of *Noye,*
And he stood eek in Iupartye
Of *timor mortis conturbat me.*　　　　　40

ffroom our forn *ffadir* this venym cam,
ffyndyng nevir noon obstacle,
Melchisedech nor of *Abraham,*
Ageyn this poyson by noon pyacle;
but of his seed ther sprang tryacle, —　　45
ffigure of *Isaak,* ye may rede and see,
Restoore to lyff by hih myracle,
Whan *timor mortis conturbat me.*

Moyses with his face bryght,
Which cleer as ony sunne shoon;　　　　50
Josue, that was so good a knyght,
that heng the kynges of *Gabaoon;*
Nor the noble myghty *Gedeoon;*
had no poweer nor no powste
ffor ther ffamous hih renon　　　　　　55
Agayn *timor mortis conturbat me.*

Sampson that rent the lion
On pecis smale thus stood the caas;
For *dauid* that slowh the champyon, —
I meene the myghty greet *Golias;*　　　60

Nor *machabeus*, the strong *Iudas*, —
Ther fatal ende whoo so lyst see, —
bothe of *Cymon* and *Ionathas*
Was *timor mortis conturbat me.*

In the *Apocalips* of Seyn *Iohn*, —   65
The chapitlys whoo so can devyde, —
the *apoostyl* thoughte that he sawh Oon
Vpon a paale hors did ryde
that poweer hadde on eu*er*y syde;
his name was deth thorugh cruelte;   70
his strook whoo so that durste abyde
Was timor mortis conturbat me.

Rekne alle the wourthy *nyne;*
And these Olde Conquerours;
Deth them made echoon to fyne,   75
And with his dedly mortal shours
Abatyd hath ther fressh flours,
And cast hem don froom hih degree;
And eek these myghty *Empours*
Seith *timor mortis conturbat me.*   80

fol. 130^b   These ladyes that were so fressh of face,
And of bewte moost souereyn :
Ester, Iudith, and eek *Candace,*
Alceste, dido, and fayr *Eleyne,*
And eek the goodly wywes tweyne   85
Maroya and *penelope*
Were embracyd in the cheyne
Of *timor mortis conturbat me.*

What may all*e* wourldly good avaylle, —
Strengthe, konnyng and rychesse?   90
For victorye in bataylle,
ffame, conquest, nor hardynesse,

kyngda*m*mys to wynne or oppresse,
Youthe, helthe nor prosperyte:
All this hath here no sykirnesse   95
Ageyn *timor mortis conturbat me.*

Whan youthe hath doon his passage,
And lusty yeerys been agoon,
Thanne folwith afftir crookyd age,
Slak skyn and many a wery boon;   100
The su*n*ne is dirk that whyloom shoon
Of lusty youthe and fressch bewte;
Whan othir socour is ther noon,
But *timor mortis conturbat me.*

fol. 131   In August whan the levys falle,   105
Wyntir folwith afftir soone
The grene of somyr doth appalle.
the wourld is changeable as the *moone;*
Than is there no moore to doone
But p*r*ovidence in ech degree   110
Of recure whan ther is no boone
Saaff *timor mortis conturbat me.*

Ech man be war and wys beforn,
Or sodeyn deth come hym to saylle;
ffor there was nevir so myghty born,   115
Armyd in platys nor in maylle,
That whan deth doth hym assaylle
hath of diffence no liberte
to thynke a fore what myght avaylle
On *timor mortis conturbat me.*   120

Empreente this mateer in your mynde,
And remembre wel on this lesson:
Al wourldly good shal leve be hynde,
Tresour and greet pocession.

Ine sodeyn transmutacion   125
ther may no bettir socour be
Thanne ofte thynke on *cristes passion*
Whan *timor mortis conturbat me.*

PATER NOSTER IN ANGLICO

39. (B β I a 1)   Harl. MS. 3724, fol. 44.

Ure fader in hevene riche,
þi name be haliid ever i-liche;
þu bringe us to þi michil blisce,
þi wille to wirche þu us wisse,
Als hit is in hevene i-do   5
Ever in eorþe ben it al so;
þat holi bred þat we lesteþ ay
þu send hit ous þis ilke day;
Forgive ous alle þat we haviþ don,
Als we forgivet uch oþir man;   10
Ne lete us falle in no fondinge,
Ak scilde us fro þe foule þinge.   Amen.

PATER NOSTER

40. (B β I a 2)   Rawlinson MS. B 408.

Pater noster, qui es in celis, sanctificetur nomen tuum

Oure fader in heuen halowed be þi name,
  As Ihesus þi sone taw t us to say:
Kepe us þi children from synne and blame,
  That we ben saued at oure laste day.
Thi name in us halowed be may   5
    Iff we make clene oure tempil with-ynne.
  Now kepe us, fader, fro deedly synne.

Adueniat regnum tuum

Fader, þi kyngdom late come to us,
    That we may come and dwelle with the :
Thy sonne, oure broþer, and oure lorde, ihesus,   10
    Bought us þat kyngdome on þe rode tre.
    Now, for his loue þat dyed for me,
        And hath oure flessh þere in his region,
        Lete me come aftur with true confession.

Fiat uoluntas tua, sicut in celo, & in terra

Fader, þi wille late euer be done,   15
    With us in erthe, as it is in heuen :
And as ofte as we make any transgression,
    The werkes of mercy late helpe us seuen
    In oure a-countes þat we stande euen,
        So þat þi wil fulfilled may be   20
        With feyth and hope and trew charite.

Panem nostrum cotidianum da nobis hodie

Geue us þis day oure euery dayes brede,
    Oure bodily sustynaunce and gostely also,
That wheþer we be a-lyue or dede
    Oure gostely fode with us may go   25
    To make us stronge a-ȝenst oure fo,
        Euer vpon us þat lythe in a-wayte
        To take þi children with hokes and bayte.

Et dimitte nobis debita nostra sicut & nos dimittimus debitoribus
nostris

And also, fader, foreȝue oure dettes,
    To al oure dettours as we forȝeue ;   30
And when oure enemye wil caste his nettes
    To cacche þi children, ȝeue hym no leue.
    Suffre us neuer þe for to greue,

Forȝeuyng al þat ys done before;
And grawnt us grace to greue þe nomore. 35

Et ne nos inducas in temptacionem

And lede us not, fader, in-to temptacion,
Ne suffre us neuer to falle þer-ynne.
The fende bryngeth us fals delectacion;
Our flessh is redy euer to synne;
The worlde is besy us for to blynne. 40
When þer temptaciones meueth our entent,
Suffer us neuer to graunt nor consent.

Sed libera nos a malo

But, fader, delyuer us from al ylle
Thorgh þese peticiouns þat ihesus ys taught,
And suffre oure sowles neuer to spylle 45
For whom þi sone so manly hath faught.
And in oure batayle ȝif we be caught
Raunsom us, fader, with mercy and grace,
And bryng us al to þi blisful place. Amen.

HYMN TO GOD

41. (B β I a 3)   Corpus MS. 54, D. 5. 14.

Hit bilimpeð forte speke, to reden, & to singe
Of him þe no mon mai at reke, king of alle kinge.
He mai binde & to breke; he mai blisse bringe;
He mai luke & unsteke michte of al þinge.

Vroure & hele folkes, fader heouenliche drichte, 5
Alle þing þet is & was, is on þine michte;
þu ȝifst þe sunne to the daiȝ, þe mone to þe nichte,
þine strengþe non ne mai telle, ne þin michte.

Iherd ȝe beo þin holi nome in heouene & in eorþe.
þu sscope eld & wind & water, þe molde is þet feorþe.　10
Of wham we alle imaked beoð, þat is þe holi eorþe.
þu þe wost al ure þoucht ; louerd, drauȝ us neor þe.

Fader & sune & holi gost, on god in þrimnesse,
inne þe nis lac ne lest auȝ alle holinesse.
Vre neode wel þu wost, & ure unkunnesse.　15
in þine hond is michte mest, louerd, þu vs blesce.

Let vs, louerd, comen among þin holi kineriche.
ihesu crist, þin elpi sune, þe is þe seolf iliche ;
he vs bouchte wið his blod of þe feondes swiche,
& of bitter helle fur, & of þe fule smiche.　20

Al swo is in heouene heȝ in eorþe beo þin wille ;
holi drichte, swete & dreȝ in heldes & in hulle ;
ne let þu neure cumen vs neȝ þene feond þe is swo ille,
Ach bind him honden, fet, & þeȝ, & let him ligge stille.

Vre daȝ wunelich bred, louerd, þu vs sende,　25
þat bred of hele & of lif, ihesu crist þe hende.
þat bred þe monkun haueð ibroucht ut of feondes bende.
he beo vre help & ure red to ure liues ende.

Fader, for ȝif vs ure gult, & eke alle ure sunne ;
Al swo we doð þe us habbeð igruld to freomede & to
　　kunne ;　30
bring us ut of worldes wo in to alle wunne,
for her beoð werkes swiðe unwreste, & þewes swiþe
　　þunne.

Bring us ut of wo & kare & of feondes fondinge ;
wicke is here ure fare & ure wuniȝinge ;
mid wicke speche & false sware & mid lesinge　35
þu ert hele & help & lif & king of alle kinge.

HEYL, LEVEDY, SE–STOERRE BRYHT

42. (B β I a 4)   Porkington MS. No. 10.

Heyl, levedy, se-stoerre bryht,
Godes moder, edy wyht,
Mayden ever vurst and late;
Of heveneriche sely ȝate,
Thylk *ave* thai thow vonge in spel,   5
Of the aungeles mouheth kald Gabriel,
In gryht ous sette, and shyld vrom shome,
That turnst abakward Eves nome;
Gulty monnes bond unbynd;
Bryng lyht tyl hoem that boeth blynd;   10
Put vrom ous oure sunne,
And ern ous elle wynne.
Shou that thou art moder one,
And he vor the take oure bone;
That vor ous thy chyld by-com,   15
And of the oure kunde nom.
Mayde one thou were myd chylde,
Among alle so mylde,
Of sunne ous quite on haste,
And make ous meoke and chaste;   20
Lyf thou ȝyf ous clene;
Wey syker ous ȝarke and lene,
That we Jesus y-soe,
And ever blythe boe!
To the vader, Cryst, and to the Holy Gost, beo thonk and
    heryinge,   25
To threo persones and o God, o menske and worshypinge!

A PRAYER TO THE VIRGIN MARY

43. (B β I a 5)   Vernon MS. fol. 407.

Ave Maris stella, dei Mater Alma,
Atque semper virgo, felix celi porta.

Heil, sterre of þe See so briht!
 Þow graunt vs to ben vr gyde;
Godes holi Moder riht,
 Þi worschipe walkeþ wyde;
Al-wey Mayden þorw his miht,   5
 Þow sittest bi his syde;
Blesset ʒate of heuene liht,
 Þow rede vs riht to ryde!
  Ladi, we ben maked al glad:
   ffor þou weore meoke I-founde,   10
  Godes Moder weore þou mad,
   I-Blesset beo þat stounde!

Liknet artou to sterre of see,
 To lihten vs, grete and smale;
Godes Moder ay to be   15
 ffor vs þou telle vr tale;
ffor þi Maydenhod so fre,
 Þou bring vs out of bale;
Help us in-to heuene fle
 Out of þis wopes dale.   20
  Ladi, bring vs out of wo!
   ffrom Bales þou vs borwe!
  Godes Moder and Mayden also,
   Þou saue vs out of sorwe!

Sumens illud Aue Gabrielis ore,
 ffunda nos in pace, mutans nomen eue.
Takyng þat word *Aue* —
 Þat sonde sat þe seete —   25
Of Gabriels mouþ so fre,
 Þorw God he gon þe grete.
Prei for us in pes to be,
 Wiþ murþes mo to meete;   30
Eues name i-tornd for þe
 Þat sit us softe and swete.

Ladi blisful, Meoke and Mylde,
  Þat word in Ioye us pultus;
Godes Moder, prei þi childe   35
  Þat he for-ȝiue vr gultus.

Aue worþily þe fel,
  Þat was þe ȝarked ȝore
Of þat Angel Gabriel,
  Þorw ȝift of Godes lore.   40
Prey us pes, þer to be snel,
  Þou salue us of vr sore;
Siþ þat Eue is tornd so well,
  Vr blisse is wel þe more.
    Ladi, qween of paradys,   45
      To þe we schullen calle,
    Godes Moder, wommon wys,
      And Mekest most of alle.

Solue vincla reis, profer lumen cecis,
  mala nostra pelle, bona cuncta posce.
Gulti bondes here vnbynd,
  Vr gultes ben to fele;   50
Seend hem siht þat here aren blynd,
  Þou bring vs to þi wele;
Put a-wey vr wikked wynt,
  Vr synful lyf þou heele;
Alle goodes aske and grynt,   55
  And sent vs of þat Meole.
    Ladi, nou þat hit is þus,
      Help we weore vnbounde;
    Godes Moder, prei for vs
      To him wiþ blodi wounde.   60

We han agult, vnbynd us here,
  Wiþ Merci fond vs fede;
Send þe blynde, lokyng clere,
  To hele us here tak hede;

Put a-wei vr wik in weere,   65
  Þat doþ us driȝe and drede;
Aske us God wiþ-outen peere,
  Þat holliche heuene meede.
    Laydi, nou þin help a-non,
      Þer of þat we ne fayle;   70
    Godes Moder, a-ȝein vr fon
      Þou most be Countur tayle.

Monstra te esse matrem, sumat par te precem
qui pro nobis natus tulit esse tuus.
Scheuh þat Moder art, enclyn
  To him þat dyȝed on Roode;
He, þorwȝ þe, tak preyer myn,   75
  Þat bouȝt us wiþ his bloode;
Boren for us was he so fyn,
  Hit com al vs to goode;
He bi-com heere sone þyn,
  Þi Milk þen was his foode.   80
    Godus Modur, þou him beere,
      Þi Milk nas non Ilyche,
    Ladi, him to fostren heere;
      Þat Burþe was ful riche.

Modur, scheuh þat þou art fre;   85
  Þe may no murþe misse;
Do þat we ben herd þorw þe,
  Þou bring us to þi blisse.
I-boren for us forsoþe was he,
  Þe synful men to wisse,   90
He þat tok þi child to be,
  Þi Mouþ wiþ his to kisse.
    Ladi briht, wiþ eiȝen gray,
      Such cos þou geete with winne;
    Godus Modur, Niht and day   95
      Þou help vs out of sinne.

Virgo singularis, inter omnes mitis,
  nos culpis solutos mites fac & castos.
One, peereles Maide now,
  Þin help adoun þou seende;
A-mong vchone, Meoke artou,
  Aȝeyn þe we ben vn-heende;   100
Sinne bond vs, þow wost hou,
  Þis world vs wol a-bleende;
Make vs meoke, cast in a vou
  In-to vr lyues ende.
      Ladi, bring vs out of strif,   105
        Vs geyneþ nouht to ȝelpe;
      Godus Modur, al vr lyf
        We spillen, bote þou helpe.

Mayden al-one, buyrde briht,
  Wel brihtor þen þe Sonne;   110
Mekest Mayden, most of miht,
  Vr gatus þou bi-gonne;
Sinne bond vs day and niht,
  We spillen þat we sponne:
Mak vs meke and clene in siht,   115
  Þen is vr game I-wonne.
      Ladi, lene vs of þi liht,
        ffor ȝit we ben to blynde;
      Godes modur, send vs miht,
        Þe rihte wei to wende.   120

Vitam presta puram, iter para tutum,
  Vt videntes Ihesum semper colletemur.
And leen vs clene lyf also,
  Þis lyf is serwe and sake;
Diht vs siker wei to go,
  Þis sunful lyf þou slake;

Get vs Ihesus to seo þer-to, 125
  Þorw siht of him to a-wake,
Vs to gladschupe euer-mo,
  Þin help vs þou by-take.
    Ladi louelich, feir and fre,
      Þou lilye whyt of face, 130
    Godus Moder briht of ble,
      We tristen to þi grace.

Clene lyf ȝif vs to-day,
  And forþward euer-more,
Greiþ vs here a syker way; 135
  We stomble ofte and sore;
Siht of Ihesu, wel þou may,
  ȝif hit þi wille wore,
Þorw þat siht to glade vs ay,
  So lyking is þi lore. 140
    Ladi al in liht I-schrud,
      Þeos wordes ben ful soþe;
    Godus Modur, Qween I-kud,
      Tak þi seruauns to þe.

COME, SHUPPERE, HOLY GOST

44. (B β I a 6)   Porkington MS. No. 10.

Come, shuppere, Holy Gost, of feth oure thouhtes
Vul wyth grace of hevene, heortes that thou wrouhtest;
Thou that art cleped vorspekere, and ȝyft vrom God y-send,
Weolle of lyf vur charite and gostlych oynement.
Thou ȝyfst the sevene ȝyftes, thou vinger of Godes honde, 5
Thou makest tonge of vlesȝe speke leodene of uche londe,
Send lyht in oure wyttes, in oure heortes love;
Ther oure body is leothe-wok, ȝyf strengthe vrom above;

Shyld ous vrom the veonde, and ȝyf ous gryth anon,
That woe wyten ous vrom sunne thorou the lodesmon.　　10
Of the vader and the sone thou ȝyf ous knoulechinge,
To leve that vel of in bothe thou ever boe woninge.
Woele to the vader, and to the sone that vrom deth aros,
And also thes Holy Gost ever worshipe and los.

A PRAYER FOR GRACE

45. (B β I a 7)　　Brit. Mus. Royal MS. 17 B. XVII.

> Ihesu myne, graunte me þi grace,
> and of amendment might & space,
> þi word to kepe & do þi wille,
> þo gode to chese & leeue þo ille,
> and þat hit so may be,　　5
> Gode ihesu, graunt hit me.　　Amen.

TO ÞE GUDE ANGELL

46. (B β I a 8)　　　　Balliol MS. 354.

> O angell dere, wher-euer I goo,
> 　Me that am comytted to thyne awarde,
> Saue, defende, & govern also,
> 　That in hewyn with the be my reward!
>
> Clense my sowle from syn þat I haue do,　　5
> 　& vertuosly me wysse to godward!
> Shyld me from þe fende evermo,
> 　& fro the paynes of hell so hard!
>
> O thou cumly angell, so gud & clere,
> 　Þat ever art abydyng with me!　　10
> Thowgh I may nother the se nor here,
> 　Yet devoutely with trist I pray to the.

My body & sowle thou kepe in fere,
  With soden deth departid þat they not be!
For þat ys thyn offes, both fere & nere,   15
  In every place wher ever I be.

O blessid angell, to me so dere,
  Messangere of God Almyght,
Govern my dedis & thowght in fere,
  To þe plesaunce of God, both day & nyght!   20
    Explicit.

A RESOLVE TO REFORM

47. (B β II a 1)   Digby MS. 2, leaf 15.

No more willi wiked be;
Forsake ich wille þis world-is fe,
þis wildis wodis, þis folen gle;
  ich wul be mild of chere:
of cnottis scal mi girdil be,   5
  becomme[n] ich wil frere.

Frer menur i wil me make,
and lecherie i wille asake;
to ihesu crist ich wil me take,
  and serue in holi churche,   10
all in mi ouris for to wake,
  goddis wille to wurche.

Wurche i wille þis workes gode,
for him þat boyht us in þe rode;
from his side ran þe blode;   15
  so dere he gan vs bie:
for sothe i tel him mor þan wode,
  þat haytit licherie.

A MORNING THANKSGIVING AND PRAYER TO GOD

48. (B β II b 1)   Vernon MS.

I þonke þe, lord god, ful of miht,
   Wiþ al þat euer I con & may,
Þat hast me sauet þis ilke niht,
   And suffret me forto abyde þis day.
   I-blesset be þou euer & ay,   5
      And halewed be þin hyʒe name;
   And worschypet be þou, lord, al-way,
      Wiþ hyʒe & lowe, wylde & tame.

In þe name of god þat al þing wrouʒth,
   Heuen & erþe and vche creature;   10
In þe name of ihesu þat me dere bouʒth,
   Þat is god, godus sone so pure;
   Þe holygost, gød in o figure,
      To þe, o god in persones þre,
   I be-take þis day of me cure,   15
      And wiþ þi tokene I marke me:
In nomine patris & filij & spiritus sancti, Amen.
Pater noster.   Aue maria.   Et Credo.

Lord god, þat þis day woldust make,
   And schope me to lyue þer-ynne,
My body & soule I þe be-take.
   Þis day, lord, kep me out of synne,   20
      Wiþ trouþe þis day my lyflode to wynne,
      So þat I do þe non offens,
   ffrom þi lawe þat I ne twynne,
      Ne breke þi ten commaundementes.

Lord god Ihesu, as þou were boren in a dawynge,   25
   Of a virgyne pure & clene,
Kepe me, lord, þis morewenynge,
   Þis day in dedly synne þat I not byn lene,

ffor wyninge of erþelyche godus :
   ffrom flessch[ly] lustus & lykynge,   30
Kepe me, lord, wiþ þi pressyos blod,
   ffrom temptacions of þe fende.

And as þou were turmentud sore
   In þat selue tyde of niht,
Wiþ bobbyng, scorny[n]ge & wel more,   35
   ffort hit were dayes light
   [. . . . . .ight]
      Sende me þis day do sum good dede
   In lettyng wrong & doyng riht,
      Þat þou, lord, mouwe quyte me my mede.   40

As þou were lord, when hit was day,
   Ofte examnet wiþ wordus grete,
Wiþ bysschopes of ful gret aray,
   Wiþ proude prynces þat þe con þrete,
   Sende me þis day drynk & mete,   45
      And susteyne me in þi seruise ;
   ȝif I be mys-hap, lord, þe fo[r]ȝete,
      Þorw þe, lord, let me aryse !

Lord, I be-take þe my fiue wyttes :
   Myn yȝen, þat I synge not in syȝth.   50
Lord, my mouth open hit in þi werkes,
   Þer-wiþ þat I may speke truþe & riȝth.
   Myn heryng, lord god, dele & dyȝh
      To here noþing aȝeyn þi wille ;
   My nese, lord ihesu, ful of myȝth,   55
      Kepe hit þat I non vuel smel.

Lord, kep & lede my feet also
   Þat heo don þi seruyse,
Þat with hem I not mys go.
   Myn honden, lord, kep on alle wyse,   60

And set hém, lord, in such asyse
   Þat I, [o] lord, with hem not synne;
And ʒif I do, lord, let me aryse,
   And let me not longe lygge þerynne.

Þeyʒ I haue syngut her-be-fore,   65
   Let me not for-garte þi grace.
I crye þe mercy, lord, euer more;
   Of amendement, lord, sende sum space,
   And sende my soule for my trespace.
      Þenke, lord, I am þi creature,   70
   And sende me, lord, help now in þis cas
      Þi mercy out ouer al mesure.

Lord, wharto woldust vengaunce take
   On me þat ʒelde me þus gulty?
I may not amendus make,   75
   But put me holly in þi mercy,
   And for my synne I am sorye:
      Þenk, of my self no myʒth I haue;
   But þou me help, in synne I dye:
      Þi grace, mercy, lord, may me saue.   80

My soule, my body, lord god ihesu,
   I now by-take in þi kepynge:
Kepe me, lord, in þi vertu,
   In al my werk & al my worchynge.
   In þi nome be al my doynge!   85
      In þe nome of Ihesu I be-gynne:
   Lord god ihesu al weldynge,
      Þis day kepe me out of synne! Amen!

AN ORISOUN TO GOD

49. (B β II b 2)   Vernon MS.

   Lord, my God al Merciable,
   I þe bi-seche wiþ herte stable

Þat I mouwe euere wilne þat þing
Þat most may beo to þy lykyng,
And wysliche folewen euere þi wille,   5
Sikerliche knowen and folfulle
Þe louereden of þi nome and blis,
Mi stat ordeynen as þi wille is.
Al þin askyng and þi wille
Euere do me, lord, folfille;   10
As me may most in soule nede
Þi wissynge help to spede.
Mi wei to þe beo siker and riht,
And harde i-fastnet wiþ þi miht,
Þat I in weole þe þonke so   15
And euere beo pacient in wo,
Þat I falle ne neuer mo
In nouþur of hem boþe two;
Ne þat I neuere glad ne be
But in þing þat lykeþ þe,   20
Ne serwe neuere bote for þing
Þat torne þe to mis-lykyng,
Ne þat I neuere desire to plesen
No mon falsliche ne displesen
Bote þe, deore lord, al-one,   25
ffor no drede of monnes mone.
Al erþliche þing beo vyl to me,
Lord, for þe loue of þe,
And alle þinges þat þyne be
Leof and deore mak hem me,   30
And þou al-one, Almihti kyng,
Out and ouer al oþur þyng
Euer beo most in my lykyng,
And wiþ me derworþest ouer alle þing.
Alle Ioyes beo nuyous to me   35
Þat ben, lord, wiþ-outen þe.
In alle trauayles þat ben for þe

Euer-more al my lykyng be.
Restes alle þat ne ben in þe,
Anuy and trauayle beo þei to me.   40
Euere myn herte to þe þou dresse,
Mi sunne to clanse wiþ serefulnesse.
   Boxum me make wiþ-oute feyning,
And glad wiþ-outen ryotyng,
Serwhful wiþ-outen þat luþer last   45
To maken of my-self out-cast,
Meur wiþ-outen greuoushed,
And Murie wiþ-outen wyldehed,
Soþ wiþ-outen falshed
Or eny oþur doublehed   50
Of fikel word wiþ double entente
To bleenden þat þe sawe mente,
Dredful wiþ-outen wonhope;
And trust wiþ-outen ouer-hope;
Min euencristne to vndurnyme so   55
Þat þer ne beo no feynyng to,
And wiþ-outen eny pruyde
Hem to edefyen in alle tyde,
In word, ensaumple, and in dede,
To alle gode from alle quede;   60
Vmble wiþ-outen ȝein-siggyng,
Suffraunt wiþ-outen grucchyng.
Waker herte ȝif þou me,
Euere, lord, a-bouten þe,
Þat neuer non oþur curiousete   65
Ne led my herte fromward þe.
ȝif me herte so noble and fre
Þat no fals loue hit drawe fro þe.
ȝif me herte þat neuermore fayle,
Ne bi conqueret in no trauayle.   70
ffreo herte, lord, ȝif me wiþ wynne,
Þat vuel delyt naue kalange Inne.

Rihtful herte ȝif me also
Þat no wrong wit ne enclyne to.
Lord, ffadur of alle Merci,   75
I þe bi-seche hertely
Cunnynge, þe to knowe ariht
Wiþ bisi sechinge day and niht,
Wiþ þat I kunne fynde,
Mi þewes in þi lykyng bynde;   80
Perseueraunce þe to abyde,
ȝif me, lord, in vche a tyde,
Wiþ hope trewe and studefast
Þat þe, lord, ay bi-cluppe fast;
Þorwh penaunce þat I mowe do   85
Þi pyneful [l]yf mowe lykne to;
And whil me lasteþ lyues space,
Gode werkes vsen þorwh þi grace,
Þyne Ioyes vsen and wiþ þe wone
In þi glorie, wiþ ffadur & sone.   Amen.   90

MANE NOBISCUM, DOMINE!

(50. B β II b 3)   Vernon MS.

In Somer bi-fore þe Ascenciun
  At Euensong on a Sonundai
Dwellyng in my deuociun
  ffor þe pees fast gon I prai:
  I herde a Reson to my pai,   5
    Þat writen was with wordes þre,
  And þus hit is, schortly to say:
    Mane nobiscum, domine!

What þis word is forte mene
  On Englisch tonge, I schal ȝou telle: 10
In Concience and we be clene,
  Digne þi, lord, with vs to dwelle, —

Þe feondes pouste for to felle, —
    Þat for vs diȝede vppon þe tre ;
In wit and worschipe, wei and welle,   15
    Mane nobiscum, domine!

Whon þou from deth was risen and gon,
    Þen as a Palmere forþ gon pas,
Þo met þou pilgrimes makyng moon,
    But ȝit þei wust neuer who þou was.   20
    Þus þen Carpes Cleophas :
      Þe Niht is neih as we may se,
    Þe liht of þe dai is waxen las :
      Mane nobiscum, domine!

Dwelle with vs, vr fader dere,   25
    Þi bidyng is in heuene-blis,
And euure þi name be halewed here.
    Þi kyngdom let vs neuere mis.
    In heuene þi wille folfuld is,
      And heere in eorþe þat hit so be !   30
    Þe Rihtwys weyes ȝe wolde vs wis,
      Mane nobiscum, domine!

Vr bred, vr vche dayes foode,
    Drihten deore, þou vs diht.
Vr dette, God þat is so goode,   35
    ffor-ȝiue vs for þi muchele miht,
    As we schul heom wiþ herte liht
      Þat in vr dette or daunger be.
    Leste we Rule vs not a-riht,
      Mane nobiscum, domine!   40

Dwelle wiþ vs, lord, leste we haue teene,
    Lede us to no temptacion.
In eny synne ȝif we beo seene,
    We prey þe of Merci and pardoun ;

Wiþ al þe Mekenes þat we moun,   45
   We schal crye, knelyng on kne:
Vppon bere whon we beo boun,
   Mane nobiscum, domine!

Lord, dwelle with vs in al ur neode;
   Wiþ-outen þe we haue no miht,   50
Vr hondes vp til vr hed to beode,
   Wit nor weole sauereþ no siht.
   In eny caas ȝif we ben cliht,
      We con not but we crie to þe,
   In al vr neode boþe day and niht,   55
      Mane nobiscum, domine!

Ho dwelleþ wiþ þe, þar haue no doute
   ffor no synne ne sodeyn chaunce.
But ay þe fend is fast aboute
      To putte vs, lord, fro þi plesaunce;   60
   Whon we beoþ out of gouernaunçe,
      Vr flesch is frele, we can not fle:
   Keep us out of al cumbraunce,
      Mane nobiscum, domine!

Dwelle wiþ vs, lord of loue and pes,   65
   And make þi wonynge vs wiþ-inne,
In Charite þat we encres,
   And kep vs out of dedly synne;
   Torn neuer þi face from us to twynne,
      ffor Marie loue, þat Mayden fre,   70
   Whon we schal eny werk beo-gynne
      Mane nobiscum, domine!

Mane nobiscum, domine!
   Wiþ-outen þe we ben riht nouht.
What Ioye or Blis weore þat to þe,   75
   To þeose þat þou hast deore abouht?

128

In word, In wille, In herte and þouht,
  We schule preye to þe Trinite :
Out of þis world whon we be brouȝt,
  Mane nobiscum, domine!   80

PRAYER FOR THE SEVEN GIFTS OF THE HOLY GHOST

51. (B β II b 4)   Vernon MS.

God þat art of mihtes most,
Þe seuen ȝiftus of þe holigost
  I preye þat Þou ȝiue me,
Þat I may þorwh þe grace of hem
Wynne þi loue and of alle men,   5
  And euere to qweme þe.

Lord, for þe ȝifte of pite
ȝif me grace sunne to fle,
  ȝif hit beo þi wille ;
And þorwh þe ȝifte of drede also   10
Euere godnesse forte do,
  And neuere to don ille.

In wit, louerd, wys me make,
Worldus pruyde euere forsake,
  ffor þi woundus fyue.   15
ȝift of strengþe graunte þou me,
Out of sunne euer to be,
  Whiles icham a-lyue.

In-sihte ȝif þou me also
Þe to knowe, in weole & wo   20
  Wheþer þat i beo Inne.
ȝift of counseil put in me
Euere for to serue þe
  Clene wiþ-oute synne.

Sende me wisdam, forte se   25
Mi wrecchednesse and my frelete
   Now and eueri day;
So þat at my lyues ende
To þat Ioye þow me sende
   Þat lasteþ now and ay.   Amen.   30

ORATIO MAGISTRI RICHARDI DE CASTRE, QUAM IPSE POSUIT

52. (B β II c 1)   Lambeth MS. 853.

Ihesu, lord, þat madist me,
   And wiþ þi blessid blood hast bouȝt,
Forȝeue þat y haue greued þee
   With worde, with wil, And eek with þouȝt.

Ihesu, in whom [is] al my trust,   5
   Þat deied upon þe roode tree,
Withdrawe myn herte from fleischli lust,
   And from al wordli vanyte!

Ihesu, for þi woundis smerte
   On feet & on þin hondis two,   10
Make me meeke & low of herte,
   And þee to loue as y schulde do!

Ihesu, for þi bitter wounde
   Þat wente to þin herte roote,
For synne þat haþ myn herte bounde,   15
   Þi blessid bloode mote be my bote.

And ihesu crist, to þee y calle
   Þat art god ful of myȝt;
Kepe me cleene, þat y ne falle
   In deedli synne neiþer be day ne nyȝt.   20

K

Ihesu, graunte me myne askinge,
    Perfite pacience in my disese,
And neuere mote y do þat þing
    Þat schulde þee in ony wise displese.

Ihesu, þat art oure heuenli king,   25
    Sooþefast god, & man also,
ȝeue me grace of good eendinge,
    And hem þat Y am holden vnto.

Ihesu, for þe deedly teeris
    Þat þou scheeddist for my gilt,   30
Here & spede my praiers,
    And spare me þat y be not spilt.

Ihesu, for them y þe biseche
    Þat wraþþen þee in ony wise,
With-holde from hem þin hond of wreche,   35
    And lete hem lyue in þi seruice.

Ihesu, moost coumfort for to se
    Of þi seintis euerychoone,
Coumfort hem þat careful been,
    And helpe hem þat ben woo bigoon.   40

Ihesu, keepe hem þat been goode,
    And ameende hem þat han greued þee,
And sende hem fruytis of erþeli fode
    As ech man nediþ in his degree.

Ihesu, þat art with-outen lees   45
    Almyȝti god in trynyte,
Ceesse þese werris, & sende us pees
    Wiþ lastinge loue & charitee.

Ihesu, þat art þe goostli stoon
Of al holi chirche in myddil erþe,   50
Bringe þi fooldis & flockis in oon,
And rule hem riȝtli with oon hirde.

Ihesu, for þi blessidful blood,
Bringe, if þou wolt, þo soulis to blis
For whom y haue had ony good,   55
And spare þat þei han do a-mys.   Amen.

HYMN TO JESUS CHRIST

53. (B β II c 2)   Thornton MS.

Ihesu Criste, Saynte Marye sonne,
Thurgh whaym þis werlde was worthily wroghte,
I pray þe come and in me wonne,
And of all filthes clense my thoghte.

Ihesu Criste, my Godde verray,   5
Þat of oure dere lady was borne,
Þou helpe now, and euer, and aye,
And lat me neuer for syn be lorne!

Iesu Criste, Goddes sone of heuen,
Þat for me dyede one þe rude,   10
I pray þe here my symple steuen,
Thurghe þe vertue of thi haly blude.

Ihesu Christ, þat one þe thirde daye,
ffra dede to lyffe rase thurgh thi myghte,
Þou gyffe me grace the serue to paye   15
And þe to wirchipe day and nyghte.

Ihesu of whaym all gudnes sprynges,
Whaym all men awe to lufe by righte,

Thou make me to ȝeme thi biddynges,
And thaym fullfill with all my myghte. 20

Ihesu Crist, þat tholede for me
Paynes and angers bitter and felle,
Late me neuer be partede fra þe,
Ne thole þe bitter paynes of helle!

Ihesu Criste, welle of mercy, 25
Of pete and of all gudnes,
Of all þe synnes þat euer did I,
I pray þe gyffe me forgyffnes.

Ihesu, to þe I make my mane;
Ihesu, to þe I calle & crye, 30
Late neuer my saule with syn be slane
ffor þe mekillness of þi mercy.

Ihesu, þat es my saueoure,
Þou be my joy and my solace,
My helpe, my hele, my comfortoure, 35
And my socoure in ilke a place.

Ihesu, þat with thi blude me boghte,
Ihesu, þou make me clene of syn,
And with þi lufe þou wounde my thoghte,
And late me neuer mare fra þe twynne. 40

Ihesu I couayte to lufe the,
And þat es hally my ȝernynge;
Þare-fore to lufe þe þou lere me,
And I thi lufe sall [euer] synge.

Ihesu, thi lufe in-to me sende, 45
And with thi lufe þou me ffede,
Ihesu, þi lufe ay in me lende,
Thi lufe euer be my saule mede.

Ihesu, my herte with lufe þou lyghte;
Thi lufe me make euer to forsake   50
All werldly joy, bathe day and nyghte,
And joy in þe anely to make.

Ihesu, þi lufe me chaufe with-in,
So þat na thynge bot the I seke;
In thi lufe make my saule to brynne,   55
Thi lufe me make bathe milde and meke.

Ihesu, my joy and my louynge,
Ihesu, my comforthe clere,
Ihesu my Godde, Ihesu my kynge,
Ihesu with-owtten pere!   60

Ihesu, þat all hase made of noghte,
Ihesu, þat boghte me dere,
Ihesu, joyne þi lufe in my thoghte
Swa þat þay neuer be sere!

Ihesu, my dere, and my drewrye,   65
Delyte þou arte to synge!
Ihesu, my myrthe, and my melodye,
In-to thi lufe me brynge!

Ihesu, Ihesu, my hony swete,
My herte, my comforthynge!   70
Ihesu, all my bales þou bete,
And to þi blysse me brynge!

Ihesu, in thi lufe wounde my thoghte,
And lyfte my herte to the!
Ihesu, my saule þat þou dere boghte,   75
Thi lufere mak it to bee!

Now Ihesu, Lorde, þou gyffe me grace,
If it be thi will,
That I may come vn-to thi place,
And wonn ay with the stylle.   Amen.   80

ALYA CANTICA

54. (B β II c 3) Trinity Coll. Cambridge, MS. B. 10. 12.

Ihesu, þi name honourde myȝt be
 wiþ al þat any lyfe is in,
Nou, swet ihesu, als þou made me,
 þou kepe me ay fro dedely synne!
Ihesu, þe sone of mary fre,   5
 þe joy of heuen þou graunt me wynne;
My saule, ihesu, take I to þe
 when my body & it sal twynne.

Ihesu, þi name in me be sett
 als þou art kynnge & lorde of lyght,   10
& graunt me grace ai bett & bett
 my lyfe to mende & lyf ay ryght.
Ihesu, þi sydes wiþ blode war wett,
 & dulefully for me war dyght;
þou kepe me oute of syne & dett,   15
 now, swete ihesu, ay moste of myght!

Ihesu, þi name is hegh to neuen,
 & ȝit I, katyfe, cry & kall,
Ihesu, me helpe & brynge to heuen
 With þe to won my synful sall.   20
Myghty ihesu, þou here my steuen
 als þou me boght when I was thrall,
& forgyfe me þe synnes seuen,
 for I am gilty in þaim all.

Ihesu, my lufe & my lykynge,   25
 for euere more blyste mot þou be.
Mi lufely lorde, my dere darlynge,
 ful wer me [fayne] myght I þe se,

Ihesu, my lorde, þou gar me synge,
    a lufely kynge is comen to me;   30
my swete swetness of alkyn thynge,
    my hope & tryste is al in þe.

Ihesu, me helpe euere more at nede,
    & fro þe fende þou me defende ;
þou sett my saule in lufe & drede,   35
    & al my myse þat I may mende.
Ihesu, þi blude þat þou walde blede,
    fro þis fals lyfe or þat I wende
þou wesche a way al my mysdede,
    & graunt me blyse with outen ende. Amen.   40

AN ORISOUN TO ÞE FYUE WOUNDES OF IHESUS CRISTUS

55. (B β II c 4)   Vernon MS.

Ihesus, þat diȝedest vppon þe tre
And þoledest deþ for loue of me
    And for myn elder sake,
ffrom þe deuel and al his miht
Þow kepe me, boþe day and niht,   5
    Wher I slepe or wake.

Lord, ȝif me grace to worche þi wille
And þi Comaundement to forþfille,
    Þat heuene may beo my Meede.
Ihesu, bring me to þi Reste,   10
Þat euere wiþ-outen ende schal leste,
    And help me at al my nede.

Now, God, þat died on þe Rode
And þer-on schedde þin herte-blode,
    And of Marie was boren,   15

Heer me whon I to þe calle,
And let me neuere in synne falle,
   Ne for my mis-dede be loren.

Ihesu, þi fyue woundes on þe Roode
Þat þou þoledest for monnes goode,   20
   Moot my socour be.
In þe worschipe of þi wounde
Þat þyn herte þolede in þat stounde,
   A Pater noster sei we. *Pater.*

In þe worschipe of þi riht honde   25
Þat was woundet in þe holy londe
   And nayled to þe tre,
Heere to-day my preyere,
As wis as þou bouhtest me dere
   Haue Merci, lord, on me. *Pater.*   30

Ihesu lord, þat is so Mylde,
ffrom dedly synne þou me schilde
   Boþe day and niht;
Cumforte me, Ihesu, wiþ þi sonde,
As wisliche as þi luft honde   35
   Was nayled wiþ on-riht. *Pater.*

God, schilde my soule þat day fro care
Whon hit schal from my bodi fare;
   Haue Merci, lord, on me,
As wis as I leue wel and wot   40
Þat on þe goode ffriday þi riht fot
   Was nayled to þe tre. *Pater.*

As wis as harde to þe tre
Þi lift ffoot was nayled for me,
   Graunte me þi grace,   45

Þat I may haue þi Ioyful reste,
Þat wiþ-outen ende schal leste
And seo þi louely face. Amen. *Pater.*

A PREYER TO ÞE FIUE WOUNDES

56. (B β II c 5)   Vernon MS.

Ihesu crist, my lemmon swete,
Þat diȝedest on þe Rode-tre,
Wiþ al my miht i þe be-seche,
ffor þi woundes two and þre,
Þat also faste mot þi loue   5
In to myn herte ficched be
As was þe spere in to þin herte
Whon þou soffredest deþ for me.

Ihesus þat diȝedest on þe Rode
    ffor þe loue of me,   10
And bouhtest me wiþ þi blode,
    Þou haue Merci of me:
What me letteþ of eny þing
    ffor to loue þe,
Beo hit me lef, beo hit me loþ,   15
    Þow do hit a-wey from me. Amen.

INVOCATION TO THE CROSS

57. (B β II c 6)   Rawlinson MS. B 408.

✠ of ihesu criste be euer oure spede,
    And kepe vs from perel of synnes and payne.
Blessid be þat lorde þat on þe crosse dide blede,
    Crist, god and man, þat for vs was slayne:
Dede he was and rose vp agayne.   5

Euer helpe us, crosse, with hym to a-ryse
Fro deeth to lyue, and synne to dispise.

Gracyous crosse, now grawnt us þat grace
   Hym for to worship with al oure mynde,
In wordes, in werkes, and in euery place   10
   Knelyng and kyssyng þe, where we þe fynde.
Late us be neuer to hym vnkynde
   Mercyfully þat made vs to be men
   Nomore to kepe but his heestis ten.

O blissful crosse, teche us al vertu   15
   Plesyng to god for oure saluacion,
Quenchyng alle vices in þe name of ihesu
   Raunson payng for oure dampnacion.
Sende us suche grace of conuersacion
   That we may stye and glorified be   20
   Where crist is kyng þat dyed on tre.

Crist, þat dyed on þe holy roode,
   I pray þe, good lorde, with al my myght,
Sende us summe part of al thy goode,
   And kepe us from yuel euer day and nyght,   25
   Contynuyng þi mercy sauyng al ryght.
   Titulle of þi passion Poynt us saue
   As to thy ✠ reuerence we may haue.

GODRIC'S SONG TO THE VIRGIN

58. (B β II d 1)

   Sainte Marie uirgine,
   moder Iesu Cristes Nazarene,
   onfo, scild, help þin Godric,
   onfang, bring hehlic wið þe in godes ric.

Sainte Marie, Cristes bur,   5
maidenes clenhad, moderes flur,
dilie mine sinne, rixe in min mod,
bring me to winne wið self god.

TO THE VIRGIN MARY

59. (B β II d 2)   Harl. MS. 2316.

Marie, ȝow quen! ȝow moder! ȝow mayden briht!
ȝow wilt! ȝow canst! ȝow art of miht!
ȝow lyf! ȝow love! ȝow hope of blisse!
In sinne, in sorwe, in nede, us wisse!

ORACIO AD SANCTAM MARIAM

60. (B β II d 3)   Harl. MS. 2382.

fol. 86.^b Mary moder, welle thu be!
Mary mayden, thenk on me!
Maiden & moder was neuer none
to geder, lady, saue thu allone.
Swete marie, mayden clene,   5
shelde me fro shame & tene;
and oute of synne thu bryng me,
and oute of dette for charite.
Lady, for thi ioyes fyve,
gete me grace in this lyve   10
to knowe & kepe euery thyng
cristen feith & goddis biddyng.
And truly wynne al þat is nede
to me and [mine] clothe and fede.
Help me, lady, & alle myne;   15
Sheld me, lady, fro helle pyne.
Sheld me, lady, fro vilony,

and fro al wikked cumpany.
Sheld me, lady, fro wikked shame,
also fro al wikked fame.   20
Swete marie, maiden mylde,
fro the fende thu me shelde;
that the fende me not dere;
Swete lady, thu me were.
bothe by day & eke bi nyght;   25
Help me, lady, with al þi myght.
And for my frendes y pray the
that they mowe y saued be
to ther sowles & to þer lyf,
lady, for thi ioyes fyf.   30
For my fomen y pray al so
that they mow here so do
that they not in wrathe daye;
swete lady, y the pray,
and tho þat ben in dedly synne   35
lat hem neuer dye ther ynne;
But, swete, thu ham rede
for to amende ther mysdede.
for me, lady, þu pray heuene kyng
that y haue shrift & housling,   40
and Jhesu, for his swete grace,
graunte me [to] haue in heuene a place;
Lady, as y trist on the,
thes prayers thu graunte me,
whil that y shal here lyve   45
that y may kepe my wittes fyve,
With pater noster and a crede
to help me, lady, at my nede.
swete lady, ful of wynne,
ful of grace & god with ynne,   50
as thu art flour of al þi kyn,
Do me foly for to blyn,

fol. 87.

and kepe me out of dedly synne
that y be not y take ther ynne.

Amen.

Explicit.

A PREIERE TO VRE LADI

61. (B β II d 4)   Vernon MS.

Marie Modur and Mayden : Euere wel þe be !
Modur and Mayden mylde : Marie, þenk on me !
Modur boþe and Mayden : Was þer neuere non
To-gedere, ladi Marie : But þi-self al-on.

Marie Mylde, þat Modur art : And mayden hol and clene, 5
To-day me schilde and euere : ffrom serwe and herte-tene ;
Marie, out of synne : Euere kep þou me,
And from þe deueles cumbrement : And out of his pouste.

Marie ful of Merci : ffor þi Ioyes fyue
Help me now and euere : To lyuen in clene lyue ;   10
And for þe deo[l]ful teres : Þou lettest vndur þe Rode,
Send me in my lyue : Grace of gostly fode,
Wher-wiþ I may my soule : Vche day her feden ;
And of bodily godus : Mi lyf also wiþ leden.

Help me, swete ladi : And alle frendes myne,   15
And schild us here from alle vr fos : And from helle-pyne ;
Swete ladi of heuene : Schild us from worldus schame,
And from þe deueles wyles : And from wikkede fame,
Nomeliche from dedly sunne : And from vilenye,
And from alle-maner folk : Of wikked Cumpaignye.   20

Swete ladi Maiden : Godus Moder Milde,
Aȝeynes þe fendus turnes : Þou vs euere schylde,
Þat no wikkede þing : Neuere vs do dere ;
ffrom sunne, ladi, euere : Þou saue vs and were.

In alle tymes, ladi : Boþe day and niht 25
Help us, seinte Marie : Wiþ al þy meyn and miht.
I preye þe for my frendes : And eke also for me,
Þat we moten here : Amendet beo þorw þe ;
As mest vr soule is nedful : And also to vr lyue,
Marie, mak hit so : Wiþ us, for þi Ioyes fyue. 30

Ladi, for myn Enemys : I preye þe also,
Þat heo in þis lyue : Moten her do so
Þat heo neuer in synne : Ne in wraþþe dye ;
Swete ladi Marie : Herteliche I þe preye.

And for alle þulke : Þat ben in clene lyue 35
I preye þe, Marie : ffor þi serwes fyue ;
Euere whil heore lyf laste : Þer-Inne þou hem holde,
Boþe whil þei ben ȝonge : And eke whil þei ben olde.

For alle þo, ladi, i preye þe : Þat ben in dedly synne ;
Suffre hem neuere for no þing : Þat þei dye þer-Inne ; 40
Swete ladi Marie : Heom wisse euere and rede,
And do hem amenden, ar þei dyen : heere heore misdede.

Marie, for þi Ioyes : Þat blisful weren alle,
Let me neuere here : In dedly sunne falle ;
Preye þou þi deore sone : Ihesu heuene-kyng, 45
He graunte me soþfast schrifte : Hosel and god endyng,
And for his precious blod : And his holy grace
In heuene-riche wiþ him-self : Þat I mowe hauen a place.

Marie, as my trust : Enterliche is in þe,
ffor þi leoue sones loue : Þeos preyers graunt þou me ; 50
And beo myn help studefast : To gete me þat blisse
Þat euermore schal lasten : Wiþ-outen eny misse. Amen.

143

ANOTHER PRAYER TO THE VIRGIN MARY

62. (B β II d 5)   Vernon MS.

Mary Modur, Qwen of heuene,
þenk on me and here my steuene!
Marie Meke and Mylde of mood,
ffor loue of þat holy Rood,
 Marie, þat þou seȝe on Rode   5
Whon þou bi þi sone stode,
 Marie, þat Ran out of his syde
fforte falle þe fendes pryde,
 Marie, ȝif me knowynge of my synne,
And let me neuere die þer-Inne;   10
 Marie, schild me from vueles alle,
And let me neuere in fondynge falle.
 Marie, prei for me þi sone
þat myn herte euere on him mone,
 Marie, to louen him ouer alle þyng   15
Wiþ herte trewe to myn endyng.
 Marie, i preye þe, Meke and Mylde,
ffor loue of þi swete childe,
 Marie, my scheld beo aȝeyn þe fende
Whon I schal out of þis world wende.   20
 Marie, of myn ende is al my drede,
Of my sunnes and of my misdede:
 Marie, forþi þou rewe on me,
þat I þorwh þe may I-saued be.
 Marie, Mi ffrendes, quike and dede,   25
þou hem wisse and þou hem rede,
 Marie, In to þat holy blis
þer Ihesu crist him-seluen is.
 Marie, at my deþ whon I schal fare
Out of þis world, droupe and dare,   30
 Marie, help me þenne as on of þyne,

144

And bring me out of serwe and pyne,
Marie, in to blisse, wiþ þe to wone,
ffor Ihesu loue, þi deore sone.   Amen.

AN ORISOUN TO ÞE FYUE IOYES OF VRE LADY

63. (B β II d 6)   Vernon MS.

Marie Modur, wel þe bee!
Modur and Mayden, þenk on me
    ffor þi muchel miht!
Marie Mayden meke and mylde,
ffrom mis-chaunce to-day me schylde,   5
    Þat me ne dere no wiht.   Aue.

Marie, þou hast no peere,
Heere to-day my preyere,
    Þouh I vn-worþi be;
To þe I clepe and calle: 10
As þou art flour of alle
    Þou haue Merci of me.   Aue.

Marie Modur and Mayden eke,
ffor þat Ioye I þe by-seche
    Þat Gabriel þe grette,   15
Þat Ioye me kepe day and niht
ffrom þe deuel and al his miht,
    And of mis-dede me lette.   Aue.

ffor þe Ioye þat God was boren
Let me not, ladi, beo forloren   20
    Þat þi sone bouht dere,
But vndurfong to-day my beode,
Þat hit may stonde me in sum steode
    Þorwh þi preyere.   Aue.

And for þe Ioye þat fro deþ to lyue   25
God vp-Ros wiþ woundes fyue
   Vppon þe paske-day,
Beo-seche þi sone, ladi Mylde,
ffrom mischaunce þat he me schilde
  As wis as he best may.   Aue.   30

And for þe Ioye God steih to heuene
On holy þoresday wiþ mylde steuene,
   Help me, ladi of miht,
And beo boþe my scheld and spere,
Þat no wikked mon me dere   35
   Ne deuel bi day no niht.   Aue.

And for þe Ioye aftur þyn ende,
Bi-fore to heuene þer þou dudest wende
   In Murþe and Iolyte,
Bryng me in to þat reste   40
Þat euer wiþ-outen ende schal leste,
   ʒif þi wille be.   Aue.

Ladi, flour of wymmen-kynne,
ʒif me grace þi loue to wynne,
   Mayden feir and fre,   45
And let me neuer for no synne
ffor-go þat Ioye þat þou art Inne,
   AMEN par Charite.   Aue.

HYMN TO THE VIRGIN

64. (B β II d 7)   Corpus MS. 54, D. 5. 14.

   Moder milde, flur of alle,
   þu ert leuedi swuþe treowe,
   bricht in bure & eke in halle,
   þi loue is euer iliche neowe;

L

on þe hit is best to calle,   5
swete leuedi, of me þu reowe,
ne let me neuere in sunnes falle
þe me ȝarked bale to breowe.

Riche quene & maiden bricht,
þu ert moder swuþe milde;   10
min hope is in þe daȝ & nicht
þat þu me sauchte wid þine childe;
for þu nult noþing bote richt.
swete leuedi, þu me sschilde
þat ic non þing mid unricht   15
wurche þe werches þe beoð towilde.

Swete leuedi, ic bidde þe,
quen of heouene þer þu ert in,
bisech þin sune par cherite
þat he me sschilde from helle pin,   20
for þer nis nouþer gome ne gleo,
auȝ þer is pine widute fin.
swete leuedi, sschild þu me
þat min soule ne cume þer in.   Amen.

IBLESSED BEO ÞU, LAUEDI

65. (B β II d 8)   Egerton MS. 613.

[I]blessed beo þu, lauedi, ful of houene Blisse,
swete flur of parais, moder of milder[t]nisse;
þu praie ihesu crist þi sone þat he me i-wisse
ware a londe al swo ihc beo þat he me ne i-misse.

Of þe, faire lauedi, min oreisun ich wile bi-ginnen;   5
þi deore swete sunnes loue þu lere me to winnen.
wel ofte ich sike and sorwe make, ne mai ich neuere blinnen,
bote þu þruh þin milde mod bringe me out of sunne.

Ofte ihc seke merci, þin swete name ich calle;
mi flehs is foul, þis world is fals, þu loke þat ich ne falle. 10
Lauedi freo, þu schild me fram þe pine of helle,
And send me in-to þat blisse þat tunge ne mai tellen.

Mine werkes, lauedi, heo makieþ me ful won;
wel ofte ich clepie and calle, þu iher me forþan.
Bote ic chabbe þe help of þe oþer i ne kan; 15
help þu me, ful wel þu mist, þu helpest mani a man.

Iblessed beo þu, lauedi, so fair and so briht;
Al min hope is uppon þe bi dai and bi nicht.
helpe þruh þin milde mod, for wel wel þu mist,
þat ich neuere for feondes sake fur-go þin eche liht. 20

Briht and scene quen of houene, ich bidde þin sunnes hore,
þe sunnes þat ich habbe i-cvn, heo rewweþ me ful sore;
wel ofte ich chabbe þe fur-saken; þe wil ich neuer eft more,
Lauedi, for þine sake treuþen feondes lore.

Iblessed beo þu, lauedi, so feir and so hende, 25
þu praie ihesu crist þi sone þat he me i-sende,
whare a londe alswo ich beo er ich honne wende
þat ich mote in parais wonien wi-þuten ende.

Bricht and scene quen of storre, so me liht and lere,
in þis false fikele world so me led and steore 30
þat ich at min ende-dai ne habbe non feond to fere.
ihesu mit ti swete blod þu bohtest ful me deore.

Ihesu, seinte marie sone, þu iher þin moder bone;
to þe ne dar i clepien noht, to hire ich make min mene.
þu do þat ich for hire sake beo imaked so clene 35
þat ich noht at dai of dome beo flemed of þin exsene.

SEINTE MARI, MODER MILDE

66. (B β II d 9)   MS. T. C. C., B. 14. 39.

Seinte Mari moder milde,
   Mater salutaris;
Feirest flour of eni felde
   Vere nuncuparis.
Thorou ihesu crist thou were wid childe;   5
Thou bring me of my thouhtes wilde
   Potente,
That maket me to dethe tee
   Repente.

Mi thounc is wilde as is the ro   10
   Luto gratulante.
Ho werchet me ful muchel wo
   Illaque favente.
Bote yef he wole wende me fro,
Ic wene myn herte breket a two   15
   Fervore.
Ic am ifaiht bo day ant naiht
   Dolore.

Jhesu, thorou thi muchele miht
   Omnia fecisti;   20
The holi gost in Marie liht
   Sicut voluisti.
Forthi he is icleped ur driht,
Ihesu, bring my thouht to Crist
   Constanter,   25
That it be stable ant nout chaungable
   Fraudanter.

Jhesu Crist, thou art on loft
   Digno tu scandente;

Hevene ant erthe thou havest iwrouht   30
  Victore triumphante;
Monkun wid thi bodi abouht,
Thou noldest lesen hym for nouht,
  Nec dare
Ant yeve the blod that was so god   35
  Tam gnare.

Suete levedi, flour of alle,
  Vere consolatrix,
Thou be myn help that I ne fall,
  Cunctis reparatrix!   40
Mildest quene ant best icorn,
Niht ant day thou be me forn
  Precantis!
Yef me grace to see thi face
  Infantis!   45

That I thorou thi suete bene,
  Tutrix orphanorum,
Mot leven al this worldes tene,
  Solamen miserorum;
Ant to the levedi mot I take,   50
And myn sunnes al fursake
  Volente,
That I ne misse of thine blisse
  Poscente.

AN ORISON TO VR LADY

67. (B β II d 10)   Vernon MS.

Heil beo þou, Marie : Mylde qwen of heuene!
Blessed is þi Nome : And good hit is to nemene.
To þe i Make my mone : I prey þe, here my steuene,
And let me neuere dye : In non of þe sunnes seuene.

Ladi seinte Marie: Qween Corteis and hende! 5
ffor þe Ioye þat þou were Inne: Whon god his Angel dude sende,
And seide þat þe holygost: Schulde in þi bodi lende,
Þou bringe me to þat blisse: Þat is wiþ-outen ende.

Ioyful was þin herte, ladi: — Þerof haue I no drede —
Whon Ihesu crist was boren of þe: ffeirest of alle þede, 10
And þou were Maiden biforn: And aftur, as we rede.
Marie, for þe loue of him: Help us at al vr nede.

Swete ladi, þou rewe on me: And mak myn herte clene,
Bring us out of sunne: Þat doþ us traye and tene;
Wo hit vs byginneþ: In werkes as we han sene; 15
Schild us from þe peynes: Þer non may oþur mene.

Ladi ful of grace: Ioyful was þi chere
Whon Ihesu crist from deþ vp ros: Þat was þe lef and dere.
Marie, for þe loue of him: Þat lay þyn herte so nere,
Bring us out of synne and serwe: While þat we aren here. 20

Ladi ful of muche miht: Þat mylde art of mod!
ffor his woundes fyue: Þat Ronnen alle on blood,
ffor þe loue of swete Ihesu: Þat dyede on þe Rod,
Get me heuene blisse: Ladi feir and god.

Ladi seinte Marie: Corteis, feir & swete! 25
ffor loue of þe teres: Þat for þi sone þou lete
Whon þou seȝe him hongen: Nayled honden and fete,
Þou sende me grace in eorþe: Mi sunnes forte bete.

In counseil art þou best: And trewest in eueri nede,
To sunfol men ful prest: In saumple of good dede: 30
ffor loue of þi deore sone: Þou seȝe on Rode blede,
Þou help us nou and euere: And schild us from mis-dede.

Ladi seinte Marie: So Rose in Erber rede,
To þe i crie and calle: To þe I make my beode:
Þou help me at myn ende: Whon I drawe to þe dede, 35
And let me neuer falle: In bondes of þe quede.

Ladi, for þe ioye : Þat þou þi-self were Inne
Whon þou seȝe Ihesu crist : fflour of al monkinne
Steih in to his riche : Þer Ioye schal neuer blynne,
Of Bale þou beo my bote : And bring me out of synne.   40

Ladi, for þat Ioye : Þat þou to crist weore tan
In to þe blisse of heuene : Wiþ Aungeles moni an,
And set bi swete Ihesu crist : In ffel, in flesch and bon,
Þou bringe me to þat blisse : Þat neuer schal beo gon.

Ladi ful of grace : Þat heiȝe sittest in trone,   45
Loue of alle blisse : Send þou me my bone :
Ihesus to louen and drede : My lyf to amenden sone,
And comen to him þat hende : Þat weldeþ Sonne and Mone.

For þi Ioyes fyue : Ladi feir and briht,
ffor þi clene Maidenhod : And for þi muchele miht,   50
Þou ȝif me miht and grace : To come to þat liht,
Þer Ioye is euere newe : And day wiþ-outen niht.

Ladi seinte Marie : ȝif þi wille ware,
As þou art ful of Ioye : And I am ful of care,
Schild me from synne and schome : Þat I falle no mare,   55
And send me hosul and schrift : Ar I heþene fare.
                                                  AMEN.

THE FIVE JOYS OF THE VIRGIN

68. (B β II d 11) Jesus Coll. (Oxford) MS. I. Arch I, 29.

Her bigynneþ þe vif Blyssen of vre leuedi seynte Marie.

> I Leuedy, for þare blisse
>   þat þu heddest at þe frume,
> Þo þu wistest myd iwisse
>   þat ihesuc wolde beo þi sune,

Þe hwile we beoþ on lyue þisse   5
    sunnen to don is vre wune;
Help vs nv þat we ne mysse
    of þat lif þat is to cume.

II Moder, bliþe were þu þo
    hwanne þu iseye heouen-king   10
Of þe ibore wiþ-vte wo
    þat scop þe and alle þing.
Beo vre scheld from vre ivo,
    and yef vs þine blessyng,
And bi-wyte vs euer-mo   15
    from alle kunnes suneging.

III Leuedi, al myd rihte
    þu were gled and bliþe
Þo crist þureh his myhte
    aros from deþe to lyue,   20
Þat alle þing con dihte
    and wes i-boren of wyue.
He make vs clene and bryhte
    for his wundes fyue.

IIII From þe Munt of olyuete   25
    þo þi sone to heouene steyh
Þu hit by-heolde myd eye swete,
    for he wes þin heorte neyh.
Þer he haueþ imaked þi sete
    in o stude þat is ful heyh;   30
Þer þe schulen engles grete
    for þu ert boþe hende and sleyh.

V Þe king þat wes of þe ibore
    to heouene he þe vette,
To þare blisse þat wes for-lore   35
    and bi hym seolue sette,

Vor he hedde þe icore
   wel veyre he þe grette.
Blyþe were þu þer-vore
   þo engles þe imette.   40

Moder of Milce and mayde hende,
   ich þe bidde as i con
Ne let þu noht þe world vs blende
   þat is ful of vre ivon.
Ac help vs at vre lyues ende,   45
   þu þat bere god and mon,
And vs alle to heouene sende
   hwenne we schulle þis lif for-gon.

Ihesuc, for þire moder bene,
   þat is so veyr and so bryht,   50
Al so wis so heo is quene
   of heouene and eorþe, and þet is ryht,
Of vre sunnes make vs clene,
   and yef vs þat eche lyht,
And to heouene vs alle i-mene,   55
   louerd, þu bryng, for wel þu Miht.

HYMN TO THE VIRGIN

69. (B β II d 12)   MS. No. CCCXX in the Library of New College, Oxford.

Swete and benygne moder and may,
   Turtill trew, flowre of women alle,
Aurora bryght, clere as the day,
    Noblest of hewe, þus we the calle;
    Lyle fragrant eke of the walle;   5
Ennewid wiþ bemys of blys,
In whom neuer was founden mys.

So fayre, so good, was neuer non;
   Transcendyng is ther-for þi place
Aungels alle and seyntis echone;   10
   Next vnto god, such is þi grace.
   Lo, þi mekenes þe did purchace
Euer in ioy so to endure
In þi grete lande, o princes pure.

Surmountyng is þin excellence,   15
   Thou rose of prys, thou flowre of may;
And phebus lyke in his ascence,
   Natyff of blys where þou art ay,
   Lady saunzpere, þis is no nay.
Empres of helle also of righte,   20
In þe is eke owre anker pight.

Stormys ageyne of cruell syn
   That puyssauntlye us do assayle;
And while we þis world be yn
   Now, lady fayre, þou us not fayle.   25
   Lat neuer vice on us prevayle.
Entrete þi babe, so, quene on hie,
In whom to þe is no denye.

Siþ here is nought but myserie;
   The fende, þe fleish, þe world also,   30
Assaute us ay wiþ-oute mercy.
   Not comfortles ȝit is owre wo;
   Lady, to þe resorte we do,
Euyr tristyng thi grace and ayde,
In whom fully owre trist is layde.   35

Sewte and servise we owe, parde,
   To þi hiȝnesse of very due,
As royall most by pedigre,

None lyke of grace ne of vertu,
Louely lady, þi servauntes trew,   40
Entrikid wiþ passiouns wylde,
In tyme of nede socour and shilde.

Saue hem fro syn and worldly shame
That þe worship with humble herte,
And to þi son, iesus by name,   45
Not sete to pray that we not smert.
Lord, þi iugement we may not sterte;
Euere þerfor thi grace us hight,
In worship of þi modere bright.

By WILLIAM HUCHEN.

NOTES

In writing these notes I have given first an account of the poem under discussion, the publication from which it is printed, and the variants, where found in manuscript, and where printed. The classification of the variants is, with a few exceptions, original. The relationship between the various poems has not been recognized, chiefly because they usually begin and end differently, and only one who has occasion to study the lyrics minutely would be struck by their resemblance.

In the textual notes I have been little concerned with the meanings of words or with doubtful interpretations. I have considered that words common in Middle English literature needed no explanation here. In fact throughout these notes I have felt it unnecessary, except in a few cases, to repeat the remarks of previous editors; all the notes, then, in this volume are my own, except, of course, those for which credit is given. My interest in studying these lyrics has been in their provenience. By showing in detail whence the poets took their phrases, their peculiar turns of thought, and their commonest ideas, I have tried to deduce the conditions out of which these poems grew. Such a study involves a consideration of the influence of the liturgy and of French secular lyric poetry.

The chief influence discernible in these poems comes from the liturgy. In trying to show the extent of liturgical influence, and how the most common and conventional phrases and ideas in these lyrics come directly from that source, I have been obliged to give much attention to lines which otherwise are too common or insignificant to demand any notice whatever. By collecting all lines of a similar nature under one note, instead of several repeated notes, I have attempted to show how great this borrowing has been, and how the very foundations of the Middle English religious lyric were laid in the daily services of the Church. Furthermore, in an effort to make this intimate relationship apparent I have carefully avoided quoting from any but frequently used services; any parallel passages from services that were not in almost daily use I have omitted, for the content of these poems, as well as their phraseology, comes directly from the devotions that were heard, read, sung and prayed, not daily only, but several times daily, by poets who were for the most part priests and clerks in regular orders.

157

I ought, perhaps, to caution one reading these notes against considering all parallel quotations as sources; I do not mean to infer by simply instancing a parallel that there is any immediate connection.   It is very easy to be injudicious in employing quotations, and in most cases I have cited the parallel merely to show that the idea or phrasing was common in the liturgy.   When the quotation seemed to me to be sufficiently close to prove an immediate connection, and other circumstances seemed also to afford evidence, I have not hesitated to express my conviction.   In comparing ideas common to the liturgy and to these poems too great similarity must not be expected, for it must be remembered that the services of the Church were written in Latin, French and English, and also that they took varying forms according to the use of each particular church.   At the best, quotations of this nature are often not so precise as one would wish.   A reader turning from these poems to the liturgy of the thirteenth century will doubtless be impressed with the fact the excerpts in these notes give a very inadequate conception of the dependence of these lyrics upon the Church services.   General ideas, too elusive to be paralleled in quotations, detailed phrases and the choice of words too slight or too uncertain to justify a note, suggest at every turn how immeasurably great is this indebtedness.

In this connection I might add that it is often assumed that in poetry as conventional as the Middle English religious lyric, passages parallel to lines in other poems or treatises may easily be found, but that such parallels prove little.   My experience has been that it is not easy to find exact parallels, either in ideas or phraseology.   It is, of course, easy to find a single idea paralleled, but with this idea there are usually one or more other thoughts that are lacking in the passage compared, as in No. 48, where one or two parallel quotations would prove nothing, but the continuation of the parallels puts the case quite beyond doubt.

The relations of these poems to French lyric poetry have been more fully treated in the Introduction.   The influence of the French lyric was largely one of spirit and approach, and is usually too elusive to be dealt with in any but a general manner.   I have given a few parallel passages from French manuscripts, but in no case are these passages to be considered as anything but suggestive.

The full titles of all works referred to will be found in the Bibliography on pp. 198 ff.   In the following references the first number denotes the volume or poem, the second the page or line; as, E. E. T. S. 71-8, volume 71, page 8, or 2-5, poem 2, line 5.

I

From the *Lay-Folks' Mass-Book;* printed, Simmons, E. E. T. S. 71-8. Variants of the Mass-Book: —

A. MS. Jac. V. 7, 27, Advocates' Lib., Edinburgh; printed Turnbull,

The Visions of Tundale together with Metrical Moralizations and other fragments; also printed, Bülbring, *Eng. Stud.* 35 (1905), 28–33.

B. Brit. Mus. Royal MS. 17 B. XVII.

C. Corpus Christi College, Oxford, MS. 155.

E. Gonville and Caius College, Cambridge, MS. 84 (2).

F. MS. in the Lib. of Henry Yates Thompson, Esq.; MSS. *B, C, E,* and *F* were printed, Simmons, E. E. T. S. 71; MS. *B* also printed, Horstman, *R. R.* II, 1–8.

D. MS. Gg V 31, University Lib., Cambridge; printed Gerould, *Eng. Stud.* 33 (1904), 1–27.

This poem is a rendering of the *Confiteor* used by the people before the Mass. Simmons by a careful comparison of the Mass-Book with the uses of different churches has proved that the original was in French, and was probably after the use of Rouen. The Confession in itself, however, differs but slightly from those generally employed at the time in all the Western churches. The form of Confession employed by the priest and repeated by the people after him reads thus: —

Ego reus & indignus sacerdos confiteor Deo caeli, & Beatae Mariae Virgini, & omnibus sanctis ejus, & vobis fratres & sorores, quia ego miser peccator peccavi nimis contra legem Dei cogitatione, locutione, tactu, visu, verbo, mente, & opere, & in cunctis aliis vitiis meis malis, Deus, mea culpa, mea culpa, mea maxima culpa: ideo deprecor te, piissima virgo Maria & omnes Sancti, & Sanctae Dei, & vos fratres & sorores, ut oretis pro me miserrimo peccatore apud Dominum Deum nostrum omnipotentem, ut ipse misereatur mei. Martene, *De Ritibus*, Tom. I, Lib. I, c. IV, art. xii, ord. 26.

Renderings of the Confiteor are frequent enough in English verse, though they seldom follow their originals so closely as does the poem in the text. There is an unpublished metrical confession in MS. No. 27, Emmanuel Coll. See James, pp. 22 ff.

2

From a *Treatise of the Manner and Mede of the Mass*, ll. 233–244; printed, Simmons, E. E. T. S. 71–134; also Furnivall, E. E. T. S. 117–499. The treatise is a free paraphrase of the *Lay-Folks' Mass-Book*. The poem follows the general outline of the Public Confession. The first part is devoted to a confession of sin; the second, to a petition for mercy.

1. *I was vn-kuynde.* Unnatural, unfilial. Parallel passages: And ofte be vnkynd un-to his grace, 3–11; I am unkuynde, and that I knowe, 5–25; Late us be neuer to hym vnkynde, 57–12; All though we haue seruyd þe vnkyndely, 26–73. The sin of unkindness is thoroughly liturgical and patristic. Cf. the Prymer of 1535: 'Keep us from the most damnable sin of unkindness.' *Three Primers*, p. 57.

4. *þat furst me wrouȝt.* Also: Graunt merci, for þou madest me, 5–65;

Ihesu, lord, þat madist me, 52–1. This idea is found constantly in
the lessons in the Prymer; cf. Ps. 131: 'Ecce, Domine . . . tu formasti me'; also the rendering in the Prymer of Ps. 119. 73: 'Thyn
hondis maden me and fourmeded me.' Mask. II, 163.

5. *And seþþe me bouȝt.* Also: 6–19; 9–9; 21–11; 23–20; 27–18; 33–
18; 43–76; 47–14; 51–37; 53–62; 53–75; 55–29; 63–21. All these
expressions may be traced back to the liturgy, and especially to the
antiphons and prayers that were in constant use. Cf. the antiphon at
the conclusion of the Gradual Psalms: 'Parce domine, parce populo tuo
quem redemisti precioso sanguine tuo,' which is rendered in the Prymer:
'Spare lord, spare to thi peple, *that thou hast bouȝt with thi precious blood.*'
Mask. II, 95. The ultimate source of the idea is scriptural, cf. Acts 20.
28: 'quam acquisivit sanguine suo,' *which he hath purchased with his
blood* — but the English poet took the phrase from the words which he
heard daily in the services.

7. *perfore.* Cf. *ideo deprecor* of the Public Confession.

10. *Graunte vs lyue.* Also: 3–7; 5–60; 21–refrain; 22–28; 25–89;
48–68. These phrases are all translations from the general absolution
employed directly after the Public Confession. Cf. the York use: 'Ab-
solutionem et remissionem omnium peccatorum vestrorum, spatium
verae paenitentiae . . . tribuat vobis omnipotens et misericors Dominus.' Surtees Soc. 59–166.

3

Printed, Clark, E. E. T. S. 129–8. The extended confessions found
so widely in the Prymers and religious treatises of the period became
somewhat conventionalized in the thirteenth century or before. It is
impossible to say just what liturgical model the poet may have had before
him, but the following excerpts from a prose confession in a 'Prymer
of Salysbury vse — newly enprynted at Rowen. M.ccccc.xxx.viij,' will
suggest the nature of these conventional rehearsals of sin: —

'The forme of confessyon.

'Fyrst, I knowlege my selfe gylty unto Almyghty God, unto our lady
saynt Mary: and to all the company of heuen . . . that . . . I haue
offended my lord God greuously, and specially in the seuen deedly synnes.
. . . I haue synned in pryde of herte . . . in pryde of clotynge: in
strength: in eloquence: in beaute: in proude wordes. . . . Also I
haue synned in enuy . . . wrathe . . . slouthe . . . couetyse. . . .
Also I haue synned in brekynge of the commaundements. I haue not
loued my lorde God aboue all thynge, nor my neyghbours as myselfe.
. . . Ferthermore I haue synned in myspendyng of my v. wyttes. . . .
Also I haue synned in not fulfyllynge of the vii werkes of mercy bodyly.
. . . Also . . . in not fulfyllyng the vii werkes of mercy spirytuall. . . .

161

Also I haue not used the gyftes of the holy Goost to the honour of God.
. . . Also I haue not gyuen tankes to our Lorde for the vii. sacramentes.'
Mask. II, 274–278.

Metrical renderings of such confessions, or of separate portions of them,
are frequent. With No. 3 should be grouped the following poems not
printed in this collection:

An orisoun for negligens of þe X Comaundemens. E. E. T. S. 98–36.
A Confession for negligence of þe dedes of mercy. E. E. T. S. 98–34.
An orysoun for sauynge of þe fyue wyttes. Ibid. 35.
Dunbar's Tabill of Confessioun. Schipper, Denksch. d. wien. Akad.,
42–56.

This kind of verse-making seems to have been regarded as a sort of religious duty. Even as gifted a poet as Dunbar failed to give it literary
merit. Such poems are interesting, however, as showing how ideas first
expressed in the sermons and treatises of the Fathers, and then established in the devotions of the people, were incorporated into this form of
poetry, and were later taken over into more permanent and higher expressions of thought in the non-liturgical poems; in some cases, indeed,
surviving yet in phrases found in the masterpieces of English literature.

7. Cf. 2–10, note.

10. In werke, in worde, in þought, in token. From the Public Confession. Cf. 'Cogitatione, locutione, tactu, . . . opere.'

11. Cf. 2–1, note.

12. Sweryng by his body, or by his face. Cf. the Confession quoted
from above: 'I haue customably sworne . . . by his swete body.'

18. rede, syng, or pray. Take part probably as a priest or clerk in
the services of the Church. Cf. the York Manual, Preces in Dominicis
Dicendae: 'We shall pray also for all prestes and clerkes that redys or
singes in this chirche or in any other.' Surtees Soc. 63–123. Cf. also
Blunt, Myroure of oure Ladye, E. E. T. S. E. S. 19–p. 3, l. 3, note.

34. spices, kinds, sorts; cf. Dan Jon Gaytryge's sermon: 'And of þis
wikkede synne commes some sere spyces, boste and auauntynge,' etc.
E. E. T. S. 26–11.

43. The werkes of mercy. Cf. Matt. 25. 34–46.

56. Or prayed for þem þat dide me offence. Cf. Matt. 5. 44: 'And pray
for them which despitefully use you, and persecute you.'

57. seuen sacramentes. Cf. the Confession quoted from above: 'As
the sacrament of baptym: of confirmation: of penaunce: of the body
of our Lorde: of wedlocke: of preesthode: and of enelynge.'

66. ȝif I shulde nombre þe branches especial. A common method of
classifying sins. Dan Michel divides Pride into seven boughs and the
boughs into twigs. Ayenbite of Inwyt, E. E. T. S. 23–17.

71. The subject-matter of this paragraph concerns the seven gifts of
the Holy Ghost: 'as the gyfte of understandynge . . . wysdome . . .

M

counseyle . . . science . . . strength . . . pyte . . . drede.' Mask.
II, 277. Cf. Isaiah 11. 2 : 'And the spirit of the Lord shall rest upon him,
the spirit of wisdom and understanding, the spirit of counsel and might,
the spirit of knowledge, and the fear of the Lord.'

4

Printed, Horstmann, E. E. T. S. 98–19. A variant of a portion of this
poem (ll. 1–8 and ll. 13–44) was published by Furnivall, Archiv. 98
(1897) 129 and later E. E. T. S. 117–785. The MS. of the variant is
mutilated, being a cut-down leaf, found in the binding of a book. I have
printed an amended version in M. L. N., January, 1910.

15 ff. Cf. the Confession in an Office of the Visitation of the Sick,
from Brit. Mus. MS. 30,506: 'I knowleche to god and to owre lady
seynte marie and to alle þe halwen of heuene, that I have senned, with
mowth spoken, with feet goon, with eyen seyen, with eren hered, with
nose smelled, with herte þowht, and with al myn senful body myswrowth.'
E. E. T. S. E. S. 90–8.

29. Ne ȝif þou me none mede | Aftur my sunfule dede. Also: 22–71 ;
6–29 f. Cf. the Litany after the Gradual Psalms: 'Domine, non secundum peccata nostra, facias nobis: Neque secundum iniquitates nostras,
retribuas nobis,' rendered : 'Lorde do nat with vs according to our synnes:
Neyther rewarde thou vs after our vngodlynes.' Mask. II. 106, note
96, and E. E. T. S. 109–lxvii.

31. But aftur lord þi grete pite | Ihesu lord, asoyle þou me. Also:
Asoyle me of sunne, 8–6. Cf. the absolution, Ordo ad Visitandam
Infirmum : 'Dominus Jesus Christus pro sua magna pietate te absolvat.'
Surtees Soc. 63–48.

45. Swete ladi seinte marie. Nearly all the epithets for Mary in these
poems come directly from the liturgy and not from French secular poetry.
The title of lady is used so frequently in these poems that it is unnecessary to note the places where it occurs. It derives from the liturgy ; cf.
the early use of it in the Sequentia, In die Assump. b. M.: 'tu . . .
domina es in caelo et in terra.' From Bod. MS. 775, written in the reign
of Ethelred, sometime between 994–1017. York Missal, Surtees Soc.
60–82.

46. fful of Alle Curtesie. Also: ladi hende and fre, 25–71 ; Moder, ful
of þewes hende, 30–33 ; so feir & so hende, 65–25 ; Corteis and hende, 67–5 ;
Corteis, feir & swete, 67–25. There are many more similar passages too
numerous to quote. These ideas and phrases come directly without
doubt from the French secular lyric, especially from the chansons d'amour
(Introduction, pp. 29 ff.). Cf. almost any French lyric, for instance the
one printed on p. 31, Douce dame prous et cortose et saige. The idea of
Mary's courtesy and beauty was doubtless inherent in the liturgy (cf.

Sequentia in die Assump. b. M., date c. A.D. 1000: 'Tu es pulchra Dei sponsa, Tu regem Christum enixa, domina es in caelo et in terra'); but it did not develop there. The nearest approach in the liturgy to the descriptions in the text is in a late and additional collect: 'O Marie al vertu makith thee fair' (Mask. II, 78). Even here it will be observed that the *fairness* is, as in all liturgical devotions, more a moral than a physical characteristic.

47. *Modur of Merci and of pite.* Cf. the Salue regina, *Mater misericordiae*, of the famous antiphon of the same name.

48. *Myn hope, myn help is al in þe.* Cf. the antiphon, *Salue regina* in the Prymer: 'Modir of merci, heil, swetnesse and our hope.'

50. *In help of al vs wrecches here.* Cf. the antiphon, *Sancta Maria*, translated: 'Seynt marie, socoure to wrecchis.'

51. On the traditions and beliefs that link these poems at times with the legends that grew up in connection with the Virgin, see 68–33, note.

59. *þe flour of alle, | þi sone.* Cf. '*Resp.* Stirps Jesse virgam produxit virgaque florem, Et super hunc florem requiescit Spiritus almus. *Vers.* Virga Dei genetrix virgo est, flos filius ejus.' *In die Sanctae Trin.* Surtees Soc. 63–190.

68. From this point the poem is a paraphrase of the litany. Cf. the *Prymer*: 'Seynte Michael: preye for us. Seynte Gabriel: preye for us.'

71. *Holy Patriarkes and prophetes.* Cf. the *Prymer*: 'All holy patriarches and prophetis: pray for us.'

5

Printed, Furnivall, E. E. T. S. 117–696; previously, Varnhagen, Anglia 7 (1884) 313. Variants: Simeon MS. 129^r; also Balliol MS. 354, fol. 145 r–146 r; printed, Flügel, Anglia 26 (1903) 160; also, Dyboski, E. E. T. S. 101–154.

1. For the influence of French lyric forms, especially of the *chanson à personnages*, on the setting of this poem, cf. Introduction, p. 38. See also below, note on l. 89. *her bi weste*, in no way suggestive of 'local color'; cf. 'Bi west, vnder a wylde wode-syde' (E. E. T. S. 117–658), and numerous other introductions.

8. *Ay, Merci, God, And graunt Merci.* 'I take *Merci* to be used in this poem in the twofold sense of Mercy and Thanks' (Furnivall). That such is the meaning is proved by the refrain of the Balliol poem: 'Now marcy, Lorde, & gramarcy.' These words were a favorite prayer; cf. MS. Trinity Coll. Camb. O. 2. 53. fol. 73 (James, III, 174): 'The Psalter of Ihesus is to sey ouer the first pater noster thies werdys folowyng: *Ihesu mercy & graunt mercy.*' Likewise Osbern Bokenam closed many of his saints' lives with: '*Mercy Jhesu & gramercy.*' Cf. Horstmann, *Osbern Bokenam's Legenden*, pp. 36 ff.

10. From the Public Confession; cf. 3–10, note.

11. *Almihti lord, haue Merci of me.* Liturgical.

12. *þat for my sunnes þi blod gon schede.* Also: 32–15; 54–37; and innumerable other expressions; all these have liturgical sources. Cf. for illustration, the antiphon: 'Salvator mundi, salva nos: *qui per crucem et sanguinem tuum* redemisti nos.' Surtees Soc. 63–194. Cf. 2–5, note.

18. Slightly varied from l. 13. Such repetition of entire lines within a poem is very common.

19. *In to þe, lord, myn herte I lifte.* Ultimately from the *Sursum corda* of the Mass service. The expression was very frequently used in mystic treatises; cf. *R. R.* I, 147: 'lift ȝoure hertis vp to me þar I am sittand on mi fader right hand.'

22. *And sle me nouȝt sodeynly.* Also: 46–13. Cf. the Litany: 'A subitanea et improuisa morte, libera nos, Domine.'

26. *kud.* Ball. *showed.*

30. *What eueri sonde.* Varnhagen prints *euer isonde*, which is preferable. Cf. the Balliol MS.: *What so euer thow sendyst.*

33. The indebtedness of this poem to the extended confessions is so evident that it is unnecessary to point it out in detail. The stanza is entirely omitted in the Balliol MS.

45. *To sle my soule In sunne I slepe.* The idea and the phraseology are met frequently in mystic writings; cf. *R. R.* I, 135: 'As þe apostle sais in þis wordes: "Surge qui dormis, & exurge a mortuis: & illuminabit te Christus," þat is," Rise þou þat *slepis in synne,* wakyn & rise fra þi deade."'

60. From the Absolution. Cf. 2–10, note.

63. *In-to þe blisse þat neuer schal blynne.* One of several paraphrases and translations of the endings of liturgical prayers. In one form or another these phrases have come into the lyrics from the services, usually occurring at the end, but sometimes as here in the body of the poem.

77. The familiar doctrine of penance.

83. *ffor þou woldest not þat I weore lost.* Also: *Thow woldest not þat I were lore,* 6–20; *Soffre þou neuere þat I be lost,* 16–11. The idea is often found in liturgical prayers; cf. the York Manual: 'Deus, qui non vis mortem peccatoris.' Surtees Soc. 63–40.*

84 ff. Cf. St. Edmund's *Mirror*: 'Thre thynges pryncypaly ere in Gode, þat es to say, Myghte, Wysdome, and Gudnes. Myghte es appropirde to Godd þe ffadire. Wysdome, to God þe Son, Gudnes, to God þe Haly Goste.' E. E. T. S. 26–20. Cf. also: 'Te myghte of ye fader almygtty | Te witt of ye sonne al witty | Te grace and ye gudeness of ye holy goste.' Item 1023, *Thorpe's Cat.* (1836).

89. The poet here leaves the complaint form, which he has been following, and closes with an expression of his own thought in a kind of *envoi* after the manner of the French poets in their *serventois* and *ballades.*

Most interesting is his use of the phrase, *Prince of alle pite*, exactly in accordance with the custom of the *serventois* and *ballade* poets, who in their *envois* invariably addressed the President of the *Puis* with the title of *Prince*. It is to be noted that elsewhere the Middle English poet uses *Lord* several times, but never *Prince;* in fact this title as applied to Christ is of rare occurrence in these lyrics; its use here is almost conclusive proof that the poet was entirely conscious that he was following foreign models. Another sign of French influence, coming either from the *serventois* or the *ballade*, is seen in the metrical form of the poem. Cf. Schipper, who in speaking of a poem by Dunbar, says: 'The form . . . is that of the old ballad-stanza, consisting of eight iambic verses of five beats, the eighth of which forms the burden of each stanza.' (*Denk. d. Wien. Akad. d. Wissensch.* 41–93.) The fact that the line in this poem has only four beats need cause no trouble, for the poets seldom adopted all the characteristics of a foreign model. Lastly, the rhyme scheme, *ababbcbc*, is that of the French and English ballades.

6

Hitherto unprinted. Variants: (*A*) Lambeth MS. 853; printed Furnivall, E. E. T. S. 24–35. (*B*) MS. Cotton. Calig. A II fol. 106, v; printed, Wright, *Rel. Antiq.* I, 197–200. The variants are interesting in that, though of different lengths, each contains more lines than the poem in the text. The Rawlinson poet may have felt the inconsistency in having emotional and didactic matter in the same poem; at any rate he has left out almost all the sermon and has thereby secured a greater unity.

15. MS. has *also;* doubtless a clerical error for *alas* of the Lambeth MS.

20. Cf. 4–29, note.

73 ff. This realistic manner of treating the subject of death, which is found everywhere in the religious and moral poetry of the Middle Ages, owes more doubtless to the seventh lesson of the Offices of the Dead than to any other possible source. Cf. the ideas and realistic manner of the following excerpts: 'My spirit shal be maad feble, my daies shulen be maad shorte, and oonli the sepulcre is left to me. . . . Lord, delyuere thou me and sette thou me besidis thee. . . . Mi daies ben passed, my thouȝtis ben wasted: turmentynge myn herte. . . . If I susteyne, helle is myn hous: and I haue araied my beed in derknessis. I seide to rott, thou art my fadir: and to wormes, ye ben my modir and my sister.' Mask. II, 143.

7

Printed, Morris, E. E. T. S. 49–192. This poem shows close relationship with the *Poema Morale*, as Ten Brink mentions (*Eng. Lit.* I, 206 f., English translation). As he does not point out the extent of the indebtedness, I have done so below.

2. *eirede*, fearful (Morris).

3–4. Cf. *Poema Morale*, ll. 5–6: 'Vnned lif ich habbe ilad, and yet me þinkþ ich lede; Hwenne ich me biþenche, ful sore ich me adrede.' E. E. T. S. 49–58.

8. This line is manifestly corrupt. Morris's suggestion that *wielde* may mean *would* does not help matters. It may be that *wielde* is an error for *widde;* such a scribal mistake could easily have been made — at any rate the sense plainly demands the preposition, *with. hwucchere*, such like (Morris). With the general thought of the entire passage cf. the familiar response in the Offices of the Dead: 'Mi soule thristide to god, the quyke welle: whanne shal I come and appere before the face of oure god?' Mask. II, 143.

9 and also 17. Cf. *P. M.* 18: 'Elde is me bi-stolen on er þan ich hit wiste.'

10. *awai to late ich was iwar; nu hit me reoweð sore.* The preacher of the Poema Morale had declared that such would be the case: 'þe wel ne doþ hwile he may hit schal him sore reowe.' l. 22. *awai*, alas.

18. *aȝitte*, understand; *suhðe*, sight. Cf. with the thought, P. M. l. 19: 'Ne may ich bi-seo me bi-fore for smoke ne for myste.'

19. *leihe*, lye, used on the hair; cf. Withals Dict. (1568): 'Lie to wasshe the head with, lixiuium.' N. E. D. *q.v.*

20. *tohte*, bright.

21. Cf. P. M. 11: 'Al to lome ich habbe agult on werke and on worde.'

24. Cf. P. M. 12: 'Al to muchel ich habbe i-spend, to lutel i-leyd an horde.'

25. *Hord þat ich telle is almesse-dede*, etc. The author of the P. M. had similar ideas: 'Sende vch sum god bivoren him þe hwile he may to heouene; Beter is on almes bi-uoren þane beoþ after seouene.' ll. 28–29.

29. Repeated from l. 21.

32. *i-ȝuðe*, permitted.

34. *steowi*, subdue.

8

Printed, Böddeker, 187; previously, Wright, *Spec. of L. P.* 47. On the stanzaic form see Schipper, *Alteng. Met.* p. 337.

3. *Murthes munne*, to think of, hence, to experience, joys. Cf. N. E. D. *s.v.* min. Böddeker has the note: 'Das aus. v. 2 zu ergänzende "madest" hat hier die Bedeutung "veranlassen, lassen;" "und liessest die Menschen der Freuden pflegen."'

6. Liturgical; cf. 4–31, note.

8. *luthere lastes*, wicked sins.

9. *þryftes*, fortune, condition. *þunne*, sorry, poor.

11. *meyn*, strength.

16. *fule flet*, very sorrowful.

17. *wayteglede*, 'Wartefroh, Hoffnungsnarr' (Böddeker).

29. *siweþ*, followeth.

36. *lauendere*, mistress. See an interesting note on the word by Professor George Philip Krapp in M. L. N. 17, No. 4, p. 205.

59. *Niþe ant onde*, envy. The words were frequently used together; cf. Lam. Hom. 65: 'Hwenne we habbeþ niþ and onde.' N. E. D. *s.v. min.*

61. *Lyare*, liar. *latymer*, interpreter.

68. *lotes*, manners; hence, actions. Cf. N. E. D. *s.v. late.*

86. *Dredful deþ.* The tendency seen in the following verses and in ll. 52–63 toward personification is not marked in the M. E. Rel. lyric.

89. *Careful mon ycast in care,* | *yfalewe as flour ylet for þ fare.* Cf. the fifth lesson, Offices of the Dead (Job xiv.): 'Homo natus de muliere brevi vivens tempore, repletur multis miseriis. Qui quasi flos egreditur, et conteritur,' and translated in the Prymer: 'A man is born of a womman and lyueth short tyme, and is fillid with manye wrecchidnessis: which gooth out and is defoulid as a flour.' Mask. II, 137.

9

Printed, Böddeker, 222; previously, Wright, *Spec. of L. P.* 99.

1. *God þat al þis myghtes may.* A common beginning for all kinds of M. E. poetry.

2. *In heuene & erþe þy wille ys oo.* Suggested perhaps by the third petition of the Lord's prayer: 'Fiat voluntas tua sicut in caelo sic in terra.'

3. *Ichabbe be losed mony a day.* A constant complaint, especially in the earlier poems. Cf. No. 5, which develops this theme at length.

5. *lay*, OF. lei, law. I was to blame, and I insisted on knowing and following my own religion, not thine.

8. *vngreyþe*, unprepared.

9. Liturgical; cf. 2–5, note.

10 ff. The thought that a man's good deeds, because of their insignificance and imperfection, are at best of little or no avail in the final judgment, is frequently expressed in the liturgy; cf., for instance, the response after the sixth lesson in the Offices of the Dead: 'Lord, nyle thou deeme me aftir my dede, for I haue don no thing worthi in thi siȝt.' Mask. II, 138.

15. *When y myself haue þourh soht* | *y knowe me for þe worst of alle.* Also: *Ich holde me vilore þen a gyw*, l. 29; *þof I be werst in my lyfynge*, 22–18. Cf. *R. R.* 1, 17: 'And neuer-þe-latter þai thynk þam-self vylest of all, & haldes þam wretchedest, leste, & lawest. þis es hali mens lyf: folow it, & be haly.'

27. *My meste vo ys my loues trowe.* Böddeker: 'Der Gedanke ist: Mein grösster Feind ist das Vertrauen in das mir gespendete Lob (dies

machte mich stolz und hielt mich von Gott fern).' Dan Michel says
that this sin of taking delight in hearing oneself praised is the second twig
that grows out of the fifth bough of Pride. *Ayenbite*, E. E. T. S. 23–25.

10

Printed, Simmons, E. E. T. S. 71–84. From the *York Hours of the
Cross*. The poem is a rendering of the following prayer: 'Domine iesu
Christe, fili dei uiui, pone passionem, crucem et mortem tuam inter
iudicium tuum et animas nostras, nunc et in hora mortis nostre; et
largiri digneris uiuis misericordiam et gratiam, defunctis veniam et re-
quiem, ecclesie regnoque pacem et concordiam, infirmis sanitatem, et
nobis peccatoribus vitam et gloriam sempiternam. Qui vivis et regnas
deus, Per omnia saecula seculorum. Amen.' E. E. T. S. 71–85.

11

Printed, Wright, *Rel. Antiq.* II, 226. In the last part of the MS.
volume in which this poem is found are a number of sermons by William
Herebert, a Franciscan friar and preacher; following these are a few
metrical translations, among which are the poem in the text and Nos.
42 and 44 with the following note: 'Istos hymnos et antiphonas quasi
omnes et cetera transtulit in anglicum, non semper de verbo ad verbum,
sed frequenter sensum aut non multum declinando, et etiam manu
scripsit frater Willelmus Herebert. Qui usum hujus quaterni habuerit,
oret pro anima dicti fratris.' Date, c. 1330. See P. Meyer, *Notice et
Extraits du MS.* 8336 *de la Bibliothèque de Sir Thomas Phillipps à Cheltenham.* Rom. 13 (1884) 536. See also Wright, *Rel. Antiq.* I, 86.

It has never been pointed out that the poem is a rendering of the Response and Versicles following the ninth lesson in the *Exsequiae Defunc-
torum*, Use of Sarum:

'*Responsorium.* Libera me, Domine, de morte aeterna in die illa tre-
menda, Quando caeli movendi sunt et terra, Dum veneris judicare saeculum per ignem (ll. 1–3).

'*Versus.* Dies illa, dies irae, calamitatis et miseriae: dies magna et
amara valde. Quando caeli, *et dicitur usque ad* Dum veneris *tantum*
(ll. 4–10).

'*Versus.* Quid ergo, misserrimus quid dicam vel quid faciam, dum
nil boni perferam ante tantum judicem?' (ll. 13–14).

10–11. Translated from the Response after the eighth lesson: 'Re-
quiem aeternam dona eis, Domine: Et lux perpetua luceat eis.' Surtees Soc. 63–71* ff.

12

Printed, Wright, *Rel. Antiq.* I, 235; also Mätzner, p. 51. Other
versions are: (1) MS. Digby 86; printed, Stengel, p. 104. (2) MS.
Emmanuel College (Cambridge), No. 27; described, James, p. 22 ff.

A rendering of the liturgical prayer used by St. Anselm in the Office of the Visitation of the Sick (Migne, *Patrol. Lat.* 158–685 ff.). It was thus well known, and appears in various forms in the religious poetry of the time. Anselm took the prayer from Ps. xxx, 6 : 'In manus tuas domine, commendo spiritum meum ; redimisti me, Domine Deus veritatis.'

13

Printed, Simmons, E. E. T. S. 71–200. Variants: Balliol MS. 354, leaf 209 ; printed Flügel, Anglia 26 (1903) 221 ; Dyboski, E. E. T. S. E. S. 101–62. Talbot Hours MS. Beaucamp MS. See note E. E. T. S. E. S. 101–179. The variants are not found alone, but form only one stanza of several prayers entitled respectively: 'Vnto the Fader . . . Vnto þe Sonne . . . Vnto þe Holy Gost . . . Vnto the Trinite . . . Vnto owr Lady . . . Vnto þe angellis . . . Vnto þe propre angell . . . Vnto John Baptist . . . Vnto þe Appostillis . . . Vnto þe martires . . . Vnto þe confessowrs . . . Vnto all holy monkis & erimitis . . . Vnto þe virgyns . . . Vnto all Sayntis.' The entire poem should have been printed in this group, as illustrating poems built upon the litany, but because of its conventional character I have been content merely to refer to it.

14

Printed, Wright, *Songs and Carols*, Percy Soc. 23 (1847) 76. Poems modeled upon the litany are frequently found. With this poem should be placed the variant forms of 13 (see note above) ; the confession, No. 4, also employs the litany.

3–4. These lines, forming the refrain, correspond in a general way to the *Ora pro nobis* of the Litany. The Litany of the poem follows the Use of York very closely.

5–6. Cf. the Litany: 'Bi thin hooli passioun and moost piteuous deeth: lord, delyuer us.' Mask. II, 102.

7. Cf. the same Litany: 'Fro dredeful pereles of oure synnes: lorde delyuere us.'

8. Cf. 'Fro endeles dampnacioun: Lord delyuer us.'

20. Cf. 'Alle ordris of hooly spiritis: prei for us.'

15

Printed, Simmons, E. E. T. S. 71–40; in the *Lay-Folks' Mass-Book*. See 1, note. Metrical prayers for use during the Mass are often found. Myrc (E. E. T. S. 31–10), after giving a metrical prayer very similar to No. 16, adds: 'Teche hem þus oþer sum þynge | To say at the holy sakerynge.' Cf. with this poem 'A preyer at þe leuacioun.' E. E. T. S. 98–24.

7. *bot þou bids aske, & we shal haue.* Cf. Matt. 7. 7 : 'Ask, and it shall be given you.'

8. *swete ihesu, make me saue.* From the liturgy; cf. the Response after the seventh lesson, *Exseq. Defunct.*: 'Deus . . . salvum me fac'; and rendered in the Prymer: 'God . . . make me saaf.' Mask. II, 144. The expression is of frequent occurrence in liturgical prayers and responses as well as in the Psalms.

16

Printed, Horstmann, E. E. T. S. 98–25.

1. *I þe honoure wiþ al my miht*, etc. Cf. the similar prayer used during this part of the Mass Service: 'Domine Jesu Christi . . . adoro et veneror hǫc sacrosanctum corpus . . .' Surtees Soc. 59–199.

13. *ladi of Merci most.* Cf. the second lesson, Horae BVM.: 'Seynt marie moost piteuous of alle piteuouse wymmen.' Mask. II, 10.

17

Printed, Fehr, Archiv. 106 (1901) 272. This poem is based upon the incident related in Matt. 15. 21–22: 'Et egressus inde Jesus secessit in partes Tyri et Sidonis. Et ecce mulier Chananaea a finibus illis egressa clamavit, dicens ei: Miserere mei, Domine fili David.'

3. *Welle of man and pyte.* Liturgical; but cf. as more directly to the point the vii Prayer in the 'xv oos': 'O Blessyd Jesu, well of endlesse pyte.' Mask. II, 258.

6. *Thou came fro heuen fro thi se.* Evidently ll. 6–9 are the words of the woman. If so *fro thi se*, doubtless seemed appropriate to the poet from the description of the woman's country given in the Gospel: 'Then Jesus went thence, and departed *into the coasts* of Tyre and Sidon. And, behold, a woman of Canaan came *out of the same coasts.*' (Auth. Vers.)

18

Printed, Clark, E. E. T. S. 129–11.

2. *For Maryes prayers and al þi sayntes.* Very common in liturgical prayers; cf. the rendering of the prayer, *Pietate tua*, in the Prymer: 'For thi pite, Lord, we bisechen the unbinde the bondes of alle oure synnes: and thoruȝ the priere of the blessid and glorious evere lastynge maide Marie, with alle thi seintes. . . .' Mask. II, 222.

19

Printed, Clark, E. E. T. S. 129–11.

6. *Graunt me of ȝoure merites a participacion.* A paraphrase probably of a clause in some liturgical prayer; cf. the prayer in the *Exseq. Defunct.*: 'et tuae redemptionis facias esse participes.'

20

Printed, Simmons, E. E. T. S. 71–350. Anonymous metrical prayers to the saints are of rare occurrence in Middle English.

3–4. Cf. the York Prayer, printed above, p. 168: 'pone passionem, crucem et mortem tuam inter iudicium tuum et animas nostras, nunc et in hora mortis nostre.'

21

Hitherto unprinted. No variants. Built upon Ps. 53 (Auth. Vers. 54).

1–2. Cf. Ps. 53. 3: 'Deus in nomine tuo salvum me fac et in virtute libera me.'

3. The idea of the sinner as diseased and of God as the physician is prominent both in the Bible and the liturgy.

6. *endeles mercy.* Cf. the xi prayer of the 'xv oos': 'O Blessyd Jesu, depnes of endles mercy.' Mask. II, 259.

8. From the absolution after the Public Confession; cf. 2–10, note.

9–10. 'Deus exaudi orationem meum, auribus percipe verba oris.' *v.* 4.

16. A portion of a word is crossed out and *mende* is written in the margin.

17–19. 'Quoniam aliene insurrexerunt in me et fortes quesierunt animam meam et non proposuerunt Deum ante conspectum suum.' *v.* 5.

25–26. 'Ecce enim Deus adjuvat me et Dominus susceptor est animi mei.' *v.* 6.

33–34. 'Avert mala inimicis meis et in veritate tua disperde illos.' *v.* 7.

41–42. 'Voluntarie sacrificabo tibi et confitebor nomine tuo Domine quoniam bonum est.' *v.* 8.

45–48. These lines are probably reminiscent of various prayers in the Mass. With ll. 45–46 cf. for instance: 'Supplices te rogamus . . . ut quotquot ex hac Altaris participatione, sacrosanctum Filii tui Corpus et sanguinem sumpserimus omni benedictione caelesti et gratia repleamur.' Surtees Soc. 59–188.

49–50. 'Quoniam ex omni tribulatione eripuisti me et super inimicos meos respexit oculus meus.' *v.* 9.

54. *Salve me, Lorde, of mercye and.* In a different hand, over an erasure; indistinct.

57. The Gloria Patri which follows the Psalm in the Prymer.

59. The line is partly erased.

22

Printed, Furnivall, E. E. T. S. 15ᵃ–133.

3. þe werlde, my flesch, þe fende, felly. Very common in religious

treatises. Maskell (II, 145) has an interesting note on the wood-cuts that appear before the ninth lesson, Offices of the Dead, in the printed editions of the Prymer. 'Commonly we find a woman with a child in her arms, before whom are placed the evil spirit, a man holding a globe, and a woman with flowers in her hand. . . . The verses below are:

> ' "A chylde that is in to this worlde comyng,
> Is hardely beset with many a fo:
> Whiche euer is redy to his vn-doyng,
> The worlde, the fleshe, the deuyll and dethe also." '

18. Cf. 9–15, note.

25. *To þi lyknes þou has me made.* Also l. 61. Cf. the prayer in the *Commendationes Mortuorum:* 'Antequam nascere novisti me; ad imaginem tuam, Domine, formasti me.' York Manual, Surtees Soc. 63–93. The thought, which of course is Biblical, is very common in liturgical prayers.

28. A reminiscence from the absolution. Cf. 2–10, note.

52. *or more or lesse ilke day to synne.* Cf. the famous response: 'Peccantem me quotidie.'

57. *Dispyce me noȝt, swete lorde ihesu,* | *I am þe warke of þin aghen hende.* Cf. the antiphon in the *Exseq. Defunct.:* 'Opera manuum tuarum, Domine, ne dispicias.' Surtees Soc. 63–63.

61. *þou has me made to þi lyknes;* | *thurgh synne I hafe loste heuenly mede.* Cf. St. Edmund: 'Wit þou þat when God made all creaturs of noghte, we rede noghte þat he made any creature till his lyknes bot man allanne. . . . Bot as tyte als we twyn fra þat lele lufe, for lufe of þis lyfe . . . we losse þe lordeshipe of þis worlde, and becommes thralles drerily to þe deuelle, þare we ware be-fore fre, and ayers of þe erytage of þe kyngdom of heuen. . . . Bot when he hade made vs man, and gafe vs þe saule to his awen lyknes . . . for to be ayers of þe erytage of heuen.' *Mirror,* E. E. T. S. 26ª–31.

71–74. Liturgical; cf. 4–29, note.

89. *Myne heretage forsoth þat is.* Cf. note above: 'for to be ayers of þe erytage of heuen.'

106. *þou art my lorde, þou art my brother.* Also 40–10. Cf. Matt. 12. 50: 'For whosoever shall do the will of my Father which is in heaven, the same is my brother, and sister and mother.'

111. Cf. the Litany for the Dying: 'Libera, Domine, animam servi tui, sicut liberasti Sussannam de falso crimine.' York Manual, Surtees Soc. 63–56*. The reference was rather popular; thus, Custance in the Man of Lawe's tale appeals to God: 'Immortal god, that savedest Susanne Fro false blame,' etc. Skeat, IV, 148.

143–144. Cf. Matt. 5. 39 ff.: 'But I say unto you, That ye resist not evil: but whosoever shall smite thee on thy right cheek, turn to him the

other also. . . . Love your enemies, bless them that curse you, do good
to them that hate you.'

159 ff. Cf. Matt. 7. 21: 'Not every one that saith unto me, Lord,
Lord, shall enter into the kingdom of heaven; but he that doeth the will
of my Father which is in heaven.'

170. & wot neuere whore, ne how, ne when. This thought formed the
substance of many popular rhymes. Cf. these verses of the early thirteenth
century, found in MS. Arundel 292:

> 'Wanne I ðenke ðinges ðre,
> Ne mai hi nevre bliðe ben;
> ðe ton is dat I sal awei,
> ðe toðer is I ne wot wilk dei,
> ðe ðridde is mi moste kare,
> I ne not wider I sal faren.' *Rel. Antiq.* I, 235.

The idea can be traced back to St. Gregory.

23

Printed, Horstmann, E. E. T. S. 98–29. This poem has an analogue,
or more probably a source in an unpublished French poem of 48 lines in
Bodley MS. 57, fol. 6 d. A variant of the Bodley poem, but later and of
only 13 verses, is found in Digby MS. 86, fol. 200, v°. It is to be noted
that in both the Bodley and Digby MSS. the poem is ascribed to St.
Edmund of Canterbury, author of the *Speculum Ecclesiae.* M. Meyer
(Romania 35–575) seems to doubt this ascription of authorship; he says:
'Est-il l'auteur de la prière qui lui est attribuée . . . ou bien n'avons-
nous ici qu'une traduction en vers d'une prière composée en latin pour
ce saint personnage, c'est ce que je ne saurais dire. Quoi qu'il en soit,
cette oraison n'est pas mentionnée dans l'article que lui a consacré
l'Histoire litteraire (XVIII, 253–269).' Thomas Tanner, however, in
his *Bibliotheca Britannico-Hibernica*, quoted by Mr. T. A. Archer in the
Dictionary of National Biography, mentions a French prayer, 'Oratio,'
and refers to MS. Omn. Anim. Oxon. No. 11. None of the catalogues
of All Souls College, Oxford, that I have consulted contains any reference
to such a poem; Tanner may be referring to the Bodley or Digby poem.
There is a curious similarity in thought, phrasing, and religious emotion
between this prayer and certain parts of the *Speculum;* there can be little
doubt that St. Edmund is the author of the poem. The saint wrote other
works in French, so the use of that language instead of Latin need cause
no surprise. For further bibliography see: P. Meyer, *Notice du MS.
Bodley 57*, Romania 35 (1906) 577; Stengel, *Codicem Digby 86*, p. 102;
T. A. Archer, *Dict. of Nat. Biog. s.v.* Edmund (Rich) Saint. I print the
beginning and close of the French poem from M. Meyer's description in
Romania.

Oracio sancti Eadmundi archiepiscopi Cant.

Duz sire Jhesu Crist, aiez merci de mei,
Ke del cel en tere venistes pur mei,
E de la virgine Marie nasquistes pur mei,
E en la croiz mort suffristes pur mei.

Merci vus cri, mun Jesu, mun sauveur,
Mun solaz, mun confort, ma joie, ma ducur.
Osteiz de mun quer orguil, ire e rancur,
Ke jo vus puisse a gré servir e amer cum Seignur.

Mut vus dei ben amer kar vus me amastes avant.

*   *   *   *   *   *

l. 44   Pur mei mesmes vus requer e pur tut mes amis,
Numeement pur N. et pur les autres morz e vifs:
Mustrez nus el jugement la clarte de vostre vis
E mettez nus trestuz ensemble en la joie de paradis.   Amen.

24

Printed, Horstman, *R. R.* I, 368.

25

Printed, Horstmann, E. E. T. S. 98–16.   Variant, MS. Thornton, fol.
211, v°; printed, Perry, E. E. T. S. 26–75; also Horstman, *R. R.* I, 365.
36. Grace was a special attribute of the Holy Ghost; cf. 5–84, note.
39–40. *ffor Marie loue, þat Maiden fre,* | *In whom þou lihtest, verrey-*
ment. Also: 66–21; 67–7; 30–18. Cf. Luke 1. 35: 'And the angel
answered and said unto her, The Holy Ghost shall come upon thee, and
the power of the Highest shall overshadow thee.'
41. *ladi Meoke and mylde.* Also: 63–4; 32–35; 60–21; 64–10;
66–1; 67–1; 67–21. These constantly used epithets for the Virgin are
thoroughly liturgical; they go back ultimately to the *Magnificat* (Luke 1.
46–55) used in evensong in the Horae, BVM., and in other services, in
which Mary sings: 'Quia respexit humilitatem ancillae suae;' rendered
'For he bihelde the mekenesse of his handmaide.'   Cf. also the hymn,
Virgo singularis, the first verse of which is translated in the Prymer:
'Maiden aloone meek among alle othir.'   Mask. II, 68.
49. *Mayden clene.* Also: 60–5; 67–50. All these epithets come
directly from the liturgy, where the purity of the Virgin is constantly
celebrated.   Cf. the response in the first lesson of the Horae, BVM.:
'Hooli maidenhood and with oute wem.'   Mask. II, 10.
58. *Of alle wimmen þou berest þe flour.* Also: 63–43; 63–11; 64–1.
These expressions, though influenced by French poetry, are ultimately
liturgical in origin; cf. the antiphon, *Aue regina celorum*, 'o marie, flour
of virgyns as the roose or the lilie.'

64. *Me bi-houeþ þou beo my counseilour.* Also: *Of kare counseil þou ert best,* 32–10. This idea may be liturgical in origin; cf. the Prymer, An Orisoun to oure ladi: 'Modir of chast counceil;' the prayer, however, is late, and I am inclined to think the idea in the places quoted above may have been influenced by French secular poetry, where it constantly occurs; cf. Bern MS. 389: 'Ne sai consoil de ma uie | se dautrui consoil nen ai | car cil mait en sa baillie | cui fui et seux et serai | por tant seux sa douce amie.' Wackernagel, xxxiii, 53.

91–92. Liturgical; cf. 2–10, note.

101 ff. Liturgical ending. Cf. 5–63, note.

26

Hitherto unprinted. Described, *Cat. of the Harl. MSS.* II, 177. Variant, Lambeth MS. 583, p. 54; printed Furnivall, E. E. T. S. 24–18. The Lambeth poem is 14 lines longer, and is in many ways a better version.

1–4. A paraphrase of the opening of the Creed; cf. a similar paraphrase in Mask. II, 242: 'I byleue stedfastely in my lord god almyȝhty, that is fadur and sone and holy goost, thre persones and on god.'

8. Lambeth MS.: *In þis world is hard aventure.*

9–10. *For who so most ys in assure | Sonnest is slayne And shent.* A reference perhaps to Proverbs 16. 18: 'Pride goeth before destruction, and an haughty spirit before a fall.'

11–12. *Whan thou this world with fyre shalt pure | do mercy to fore thy jugement.* Cf. the response after the fifth lesson, *Vig. Mort.:* 'Ne recorderis peccata mea, Domine, Dum veneris judicare saeculum per ignem.' Surtees Soc. 63–70*. *Whan:* the Lambeth MS. has *Or* which makes a better reading, but lacks the literal translation that the Harleian poet seems to have preferred.

13–16. A translation and amplification of the versicle in the famous responsorium after the ninth lesson, *Vig. Mort.:* 'Nunc, Christe, te petimus miserere, quaesumus, qui venisti redimere perditos, noli damnare redemptos.' Surtees Soc. 63–71*.

17–18. Cf. the response after the eighth lesson: 'Quia in inferno nulla est redemptio.' *Ibid.*

25. *We aske mercy of rightnesnesse; i.e.* of the righteousness of God. With ll. 25–26 cf. Rom. 10. 3–4: 'For they being ignorant of God's righteousness, and going about to establish their own righteousness have not submitted themselves unto the righteousness of God.'

35. Cf. 22–33, note.

38. *mercy A boue thy workes alle.* Cf. the *Craft of Deyng:* 'fore godis mercy is abwne al his werkis, and he may nocht deny mercy treuly askyt.' E. E. T. S. 43–3.

39. Cf. St. Edmund's *Mirror:* 'ffor whene we ware twynnede fra Godde, our sweteste ffadire, and be-come thralles to þe ill gaste, than he

. . . sente his awen Sonne . . . and one þis manere did he þe dede.'
E. E. T. S. 26ª–32.

48–54. Probably from St. Edmund: 'To summe, beoing wiþ-oute
more, as to stones; to summe beoing and liuing, as to treon; to summe
beoing, liuing, and felyng, as to beestes; to summe being, liuing, felyng,
and vnderstonding, as to Angeles and to Mon. . . . Men haue beo-
inge wiþ stones, Liuynge wiþ herbes, ffelynge wiþ Beestes, Resoun wiþ
Angeles.' Horstman, *R. R.* I, 245. The thought, however, originated
with St. Gregory. It occurs three times in his works, whence it was often
quoted. Gower cites it thrice. Cf. Mr. Macaulay's note on ll. 945 ff.
of the Prologue of the *Confessio Amantis.*

55. Lambeth MS. has: *þou baddist þat alle schulde multiplie. But we
ben fals & necligent.* With this cf. St. Edmund in the same paragraph
from which the above is taken: 'and thynke how it es grete myghte to
make all thynges of noghte and . . . to multyply þam ilk a day for oure
prowe. A! mercy Godde! how we are vnkynde! . . . We distruy
þam ilke a day & he þam multyplies.'

59 ff. Cf. the prayer in the *Mirror:* 'In manus tuas Domine . . .
commendo in nocte (vel die) animam meam et corpus meum et patrem
et matrem, fratres et sorores, amicos familiares . . . custodi nos, Domine
in hac nocte, (vel die) per merita & intercessionem beate Marie et omnium
sanctorum, a vicijs, a concupis[c]encijs, a peccatis, et temptacionibus
diaboli.' E. E. T. S. 26ª–19.

65. Cf. the Litany for the Dying: 'Ab hoste iniquo: libera et defende animam ejus, Domine. Ab insidiis et laqueis diaboli, libera et
defende animam ejus, Domine.' Surtees Soc. 63–54*.

69. Cf. the versicle after the ninth lesson, *Vig. Mort.:* 'Quid ergo,
miserrimus, quid dicam vel quid faciam Dum veneris judicare saeculum
per ignem?' And the paraphrase of these lines in No. 12: 'Ich am
overgard agast, and quake al in my speche.'

67. There is no such promise in the Gospel narratives nor in any of
the religious treatises that I have read. The passage has evidently been
corrupted in copying, for the Lamb. MS. reads: '*And suffre him not
oure soule away to take | For whiche on roode þou were torent.*' The poet
was perhaps forced into the assertion of l. 67, after having written the
preceding line, by the necessity of a rhyming word for *jugement* in l. 70.
With l. 67 cf. Hebrew 13. 5: 'For he hath said, I will never leave thee nor
forsake thee.'

75–76. Liturgical.

77. Cf. Mark 16. 16: 'He that believeth, and is baptized, shall be
saved.'

81. Cf. the Prayer in the York Horae: 'Domine iesu Christe . . .
pone passionem . . . inter iudicium tuum et animas nostras.' Cf. 10,
note.

27

Printed, Böddeker, 193; previously, Wright, *Spec. of L. P.*, Percy
Soc. 4–59.

10–15. The setting proper, which has been influenced by the French
lyric setting; cf. Introduction, p. 39.

26–27. Liturgical ending.

28

Hitherto unprinted. Described, Gregory Smith, *Spec. of Mid. Scots*,
p. lxx. Variant, Balliol MS. 354 fol. 144r°–145r°; printed, Flügel, Anglia
26 (1903) 157; Dyboski, E. E. T. S. E. S. 101–52.

1. *To the, maist peirlas prince of pece.* Cf. Is. 9. 6: 'For unto us
a child is born, unto us a son is given: and the government shall be upon
his shoulder: and his name shall be called Wonderful, Counsellor,
The mighty God, The everlasting Father, *The Prince of Peace.*'

3. *Let neuir thi micht be merciles | Til man that thou has maid of clay.*
Also: *To take my kuynde of clay*, 23–11. Cf. the third lesson, *Vig.
Mort.* (Job x.): 'Manus tuae fecerunt me, et plasmaverunt me totum
in circuitu . . . Memento, quaeso, quod sicut lutum feceris me.'

8. *Miserere mei, Deus.* Undoubtedly from the response after the
seventh lesson, *Vig. Mort.*: 'Miserere mei, Deus et salve me.'

10. *Sall fallou and faid | as dois a flour.* This idea is prominent in
the religious and moral poems of the fifteenth century, especially in those
which employ the *Ubi sunt* motive. Nearly all such passages in Middle
English poetry seem to have been influenced by the lessons from Job in
the Offices of the Dead. Cf. with stanza 2 the fifth lesson: 'Homo
natus de muliere, brevi vivens tempore, repletur multis miseriis, Qui
quas flos egreditur, et conteritur, et fugit velut umbra et numquam in
eodem statu permanet.'

14. Erasure or imperfection in MS.

50. *Mary consawit throw gabriell stevin.* Cf. the Prymer: 'Heil thou,
virgyne modir of crist, that bi eere conceyuedist: thurȝ gabriels message.'
Mask. II, 73.

57. *Thou lat thi pece spred and spring.* A welcome relief from the line
ever present in the poems of Jacob Ryman, and elsewhere, *Let thy pity
spread and spring.* The Balliol MS. has the conventional verse.

61. Cf. John 19. 19: 'And Pilate wrote a title, and put it on the cross.
And the writing was, Jesus of Nazareth, The King of the Jews.'

29

Printed, Furnivall, E. E. T. S. 117–755; previously in Archiv 97 (1896)
311. *A ryme-beginning poem.* Furnivall.

2. *haf pite of me and merci!* Quite in the mood of the French secular
lyric.

N

7. Liturgical; cf. 3 -10, note.

8. The connected stanzas indicate French influence; cf. Introduction, p. 32.

13 ff. Cf. the Litany for the Dying: 'Ab incursu malignorum spiritum: libera et defende animam ejus Domine.' Surtees Soc. 63–54*.

30

Printed, Morris, E. E. T. S. 53–255. Date, 'before A.D. 1300.' Morris.

1. *Edi beo þu.* Cf. the Salutation, *Benedicta tu*, which is found as the first line of many responses and versicles in the Horae, BVM., as *e.g.* after the first lesson, 'Blessed be thou among alle wymmen.' Mask. II. 10.

heuene quene. Also: 14–11; 32–33; 64–18; 66–41. All these passages go back ultimately to the liturgy; cf. the *Sequentia, in die Purif.:* 'Virgo ⁚ . . . regina caeli.' Surtees Soc. 60–20.

2. *folkes froure & engles blis.* Cf. with ll. 1–2 the York Missal, *In die assump.:* 'Benedicta tu in mulieribus | Quae peperisti *pacem hominibus* | *Et angelis gloriam.*' Surtees Soc. 60–83.

3. *Moder unwemmed & Maiden clene.* Cf. the Horae, BVM., response: 'Aftir the birthe thou dwelledist unwemmyd virgyne.' Mask. II, 54. Cf. also 25–49, note.

5–7. These lines may have their ultimate origin in the liturgy in the responses of the Horae, BVM., but they are in spirit essentially in the manner of French lyric poetry; one is tempted to say that they owe little to the liturgy.

7–8. The last two lines of each stanza form a kind of refrain. The spirit is entirely after the manner of the *chansons d'amour.*

9. *þu asteȝe so þe daiȝ rewe.* Cf. the Prosa, De Assump. B. M.: 'velut sol micans cuncta conscendisti globorum luminaria, lucerna nitens inter choros angelorum.' Date, 994–1017. Surtees Soc. 60–294.

11–12. Cf. John 1. 4 ff.: 'in ipso vita erat, et vita erat lux hominum. Et lux in tenebris lucet . . . erat lux vera, quae illuminat omnem hominem venientem in hunc mundum.'

16. *& haue merci of þin knicht.* A delightful touch — and one that shows incidentally, not that English chivalry enters into these poems, but rather that French lyrics find their truest expression in English in little echoes heard now and then in the lines of poets who have caught the spirit without being unduly fettered by a sense of form.

17. Cf. Is. 11. 1–2: 'A rodde shall sprynge out of the rowte Iesse; and out of the rowte therof shall sprynge vp a flowre, and therevpon shall reste the spyryte of the lorde.' As rendered in the *Myroure of oure Ladye*, E. E. T. S. E. S. 19–147.

22. *ic am þi mon.* An expression translated literally from French secular poetry, and also frequent in the Middle English love songs.

25 ff. Evidently from an anthem used at times in the Horae, BVM.; rendered in the *Myroure of oure Ladye:* 'Blyssed be thow most worthy sower that haste sowen a grayne of the beste whete in the best lande wette wyth the dew of the holy goste.' E. E. T. S. E. S. 19–201.

41. *þu ert icumen of heȝe kunne | of dauid þe riche king.* After the manner of the French lyric poet who was accustomed to celebrate the high rank and birth of his lady. Cf. Introduction, p. 34. The idea, of course, is here both liturgical and scriptural.

49. *Swetelic ure loured hit diȝte | þat þu maide wið-ute were.* A common theme in liturgical devotions. Cf. the Horae, BVM.: 'Oratio. Almyȝti euerlastynge god, that wonderli thurȝ the hooli goost madist redi bodi and soule of the gloriouse virgyne modir marie: that she deseruede to be maad the worthi dwellynge place of thi sone.' Mask. II, 73. *Swetelic,* margin has, *Seolcudliche, i.e. treowe.*

51–52. *þat al þis world bicluppe ne miȝte | þu sscholdest of þin boseme bere.* From the third lesson, BVM.: 'Hooli modir of god, that deseruedist worthili to conceyue him that al the world myȝte not holde.' Cf. also the response after the first lesson: 'For him that heuenes myȝten not take thou beer in thi wombe.' Mask. II, 10.

53. *þe ne stiȝte, ne þe ne priȝte | in side, in lende, ne elles where.* Cf. Horae, BVM.: 'Heil thou, for ful with god, childedist withoute peyne.' Mask. II, 74. Cf. also St. Bernard: 'Conceptus fuit sine pudore, *partus sine dolore.*' Serm., In vig. nat., 4, 3.

55. *þat wes wið ful muchel riȝte | for þu bere þine helere.* A paraphrase evidently of a portion of the *Beata es,* Horae, BVM.: 'Blessid art thou virgyn marie . . . thou hast getyn hym that made thee.' Mask. II, 61.

31

Printed, E. E. T. S. 49–158; previously, Wright, *Owl and Nightingale,* Percy Soc. 11 (1843) 65. Variants: (*A*) T. C. C., B. 14. 39; printed, Chambers and Sidgwick, 94; (*B*) Jesus Coll. Oxford, I, 29; printed, Morris, E. E. T. S. 49–159.

1–3. On the influence of French lyric forms on this poem, cf. Introduction, p. 36.

31–32. Cf. the *Poema Morale:* 'Vnnet lif ich habbe iled . . . wel ful sare ich me adrede.' ll. 5–6. Cf. also 7–4. There are other parallels between this poem and No. 7, but they are hardly striking enough to be convincing.

32

Printed, Morris, E. E. T. S. 49–194; previously, Wright, *Rel. Antiq.* I, 89; also printed, Mätzner, 53; Chambers and Sidgwick, 92; Stobart, *Chaucer's Epoch,* 15.

2. *velud maris stella.* These Latin *caudae* are reminiscences of famous proses, sequences, hymns and other devotions connected with the various services of the Virgin Mary. It is to be noted that the Latin words are, as a rule, carefully worked into the poem and not merely inserted as in-laid ornaments. The poet did not consciously borrow, culling phrases here and there from hymns, to suit his fancy, but rather he composed a poem in which he expressed part of his thought in English, part in Latin. That a few — and only a few — of these *caudae* happen to be found in the hymns proves nothing beyond the fact that the author was an orthodox church-going Christian who was accustomed to hear hymns in honor of the Virgin daily, and often several times daily. Cf. Introduction, p. 25. With l. 2 cf. almost any devotion of the Horae, BVM., especially the first line of the famous hymn, *Ave Maris Stella.*

3. *Briȝter þan þe day-is liȝt.* The comparison of Mary to the light of day is a favorite one in all medieval poetry, and owes its origin probably to the early sequences; cf., for instance, the Prose, De Assump. B. M.: 'rosa processit sicut sol. Oritur, ut lucifer inter astra decoravit polorum sidera.' Date, c. 1000. Surtees Soc. 60–294.

4. *parens et puella.* Cf. the first lesson in the Horae: 'Modir and dauȝter'; also later: 'modir and virgyne.' Mask. II, 10. I regret that I have no Latin Horae available from which to quote these phrases.

19. Cf. the hymn, *O gloriosa*, Horae, BVM.: 'Quod Eua tristis abstulit, Tu reddis almo germine.' Mask. II, 24, note 53.

33

Printed, Böddeker, 213; Wright, *Spec. of L. P.* 87; Chambers and Sidgwick, 97.

1 ff. On the setting, see Introduction, p. 33.

30. *þurh hire medicine.* With this title for Christ, if we may call it such, cf. the antiphon in the Horae: 'Suche a deeth undirȝede the medicyn of liif.' Mask. II, 64.

33. *hire erbes smulleþ suete.* This manner of speaking of Christ and Mary is both liturgical and patristic. Thus St. Bernard celebrates the 'fragrance of this odorous fruit' (Hom. iii on the *Missus est*); and the Horae, BVM., has the significant *Capitulum:* 'As cauel and bawme swote smellynge I ȝaf swoot odour: as triede myrre I ȝaf swetnesse of smellynge.' Mask. II, 68. The theme is perhaps more popular in French religious poetry than in English. Cf. for instance a song in the Bern MS. 358: 'Tu ies bames natureis. douls miels et laituaires. tu ies pimens sauoreis. pucelle debonaire. nos cuers purge et esclaire.' Wackernagel, xlv, p. 69.

34

Printed, Fehr, Archiv 106 (1901) 276.

2 ff. *peccantem me cotidie . . . Timor mortis conturbat me . . . saluum*

me fac, domine. From the response after the ninth lesson, *Vig. Mort.:* *'Peccantem me quotidie* et non repaenitentem *timor mortis conturbat me. . . . Deus* in nomine tuo *salvum me fac.'*

10. *parce michi, domine.* From the first lesson (Job vii.), *Vig. Mort.:* 'Parce mihi, Domine.'

12. Fehr prints *boʒsteste*, presumably for *boʒsteste*, or better *boʒtest(e)*.

35

Printed, Flügel, Anglia, 26 (1903) 193; previously, Wright, *Songs and Carols*, Percy Soc. 23–74. The three following poems, 35, 36, and 37, have close relations. The parallels between 36 and 37 have been pointed out by Professor Flügel, and are so evident that I have not repeated them in detail; the ideas that are common to all three poems will be found below. The facts, that in no case do the lines exactly correspond, that in only one stanza are the rhyming words the same (36, st. 7, and 37, st. 6), that the rhyme scheme is always the same, that the meter is always identical, and that 37 is a partial translation, part of the line being left in the Latin, the other part translated (cf. Mr. Chambers' essay in Chambers and Sidgwick), — all these facts are pretty conclusive evidence that there existed a number of these poems, all closely alike in ideas, all employing the same refrain, the same meter, the same rhyme scheme, *aaaB*, and quite probably written originally in Latin. With these poems should be grouped: (1) Dunbar's *Lament for the Makaris.* (Cf. 37, note.) (2) Lydgate's *Timor Mortis Conturbat Me.* (Printed here.) (3) An unpublished poem in MS. Porkington, No. 10, fol. 195, with the same refrain; described, Madden, *Syr Gawayne*, p. lxii. The poem is composed of twelve stanzas of twelve lines each, which renders it probable that, like Lydgate's poem, it has little actual connection with the typical *Timor Mortis* poems. (4) An unpublished poem in a MS. belonging to the Marquis of Bath; described, Hist. MSS. Com., III, 180: 'A poem beginning, Timor mortis conturbat me.' (5) An unpublished poem in the Audelay MS.; described Anglia, 18–211.

6. From the response after the seventh lesson; cf. 34–2, note.

11. A most popular bit of argument; cf. 22–170, note.

19. *Jhesu cryst whan yat he shuld sofer hys passyon, | To hys fader he seyd with gret deuocyon, | Thys is ye causse of my intercessyon: | ye dred off deth do troble me!* Cf. 36, 15–19: 'Jhesu cryst whane he schuld dey | to hys fader he gan sey: | fader, he sayd, in trinyte | timor &c.;' also 37, 15–17, 'Christus se ipsum, whan he shuld dye, | Patri suo his manhode did Crye: | Respice me, pater, that is so hye, | terribilis mors.' A reference doubtless to the agony in the Garden.

23–25. Cf. 36, 19–21; also 37–20: 'Duc me from this vanyte.'

31–33. Cf. 36, 27–29; also 37, 11–13.

36

˹ Printed, Flügel, Anglia, 26 (1906) 192; Wright, *Songs and Carols*, Percy Soc. 23–57.   Variant, only four stanzas, Balliol MS. 354; printed, Flügel, Anglia 26 (1906) 192; Dyboski, E. E. T. S. 103–3; Chambers and Sidgwick, 150.

37

▓Printed, Flügel, Anglia 26ʹ(1906) 259; Dyboski, E. E. T. S. E. S. 101–36.   Chambers and Sidgwick, 149.

1–8. Cf. the general content of 36, 1–8.

9. *Corpus migrat in my sowle.*   Cf. 35–15: 'Whan my sowle & my body departyd shallbe.'

Editors of Dunbar have failed to notice that the *Lament for the Makaris* is intimately connected with the group of poems represented by the three preceding lyrics.   David Laing in trying to throw light on the source of the *Lament* said 'that the refrain, *Timor mortis conturbat me*, is taken from a poem by Lydgate beginning: "So as I lay the other night."' (Quoted by Gregor, Scott. Text Soc. Poems of Dunbar, III, 91.)   A comparison of the *Lament* with Lydgate's poem, here printed for the first time, will reveal the fact that there is probably no connection between the two poems; their stanzaic structure is totally different, and their content is remarkably unlike.   It is hard to believe that Dunbar had ever seen Lydgate's poem.   Mr. Gregor evidently felt that the connection with Lydgate was not entirely proved, for he goes on to suggest that 'the poet may have had in mind the words, "Circumdederunt me dolores mortis," Ps. cxiv. 3 (cxvi. 3).   Buchanan translates, "Jam mors ante oculos erat."   Cf. Ps. liv. 4.'   He may have had such a passage in mind, it is true, but it is far more likely that, like the poets of Nos. 35, 36, and 37, he could not escape the words of the awful responsorium.   Furthermore it has been established in the notes to the *Timor Mortis* poems that there was in all probability a body of these lyrics, written originally in Latin, and all more or less closely related.   The parallels pointed out below between the *Lament* and the three poems in the text prove almost conclusively that Dunbar here, as in the *Tabill of Confessioun* (cf. note to No. 3), has taken his suggestion and general content from popular forms of religious poetry, but with a poet's genius has adapted those conventions to his own needs.   In comparing the *Lament* with the *Timor Mortis* poems it is to be observed that the stanza in each case is composed of three lines and a refrain; that the meter is the same, and that the rhyme scheme, though different, is not radically so.   In content the poems have the same general tone and the same lyrical emotion.   The resemblances in wording are not striking, though the thought is often similar.   The following parallels between the *Lament* and Nos. 35, 36, and 37 are suggestive:

Lament, 1–4: *I that in heill wes and glaidness | Am trublit now with gret seikness | And feblit with infirmite | Timor Mortis conturbat me.*

Cf. No. 37, 1–4: '*Illa juventus* that is so nyse | *Me deduxit* into vain Devise; | *Infirmus sum*, I may not Rise | *Terribilis mors conturbat me.*' Also: '*Iam ductus sum in to my bed.*' *Ibid*, 9.

Lament, 5–6: *Our plesaunce heir is all vane glory, | This fals warld is bot transitory.*

Cf. No. 35, 24–25: 'Thys world is butt a chery ffare | Replett with sorow & fulfylled with care.' Also: '*Duc me* from this vanyty.' 37–20.

Lament, 7: *The flesche is brukle, the Feynd is sle.*

Cf. 37, 12–13: '*Respicit demon* in his Rowle, | *Desiderat ipse* to haue his tolle.'

Lament, 17–20: *Vnto the deth gois all estaitis | Princis, prelattis and Potestaitis | Bayth riche and pure of all degree | Timor Mortis conturbat me.*

Cf. 35, 7–10: 'I haue be lorde of towr and towne | I sett not be my gret renowne; ffor deth wyll pluck[yt] all downe; The dred of deth do trobyll me.'

In view of the *provenience* of the *Lament* too much stress must not be laid on Schipper's statement that '. . . the general tone of it especially the contents of the first stanza, where he says, *v*. 3, that he is *feblit with infirmitie*, make it [clear] that it was written by Dunbar in advanced age.'

38

Hitherto unprinted. Described, *Cat. of Harl. MSS.*, p. 593; also, MacCracken, *The Lydgate Canon*, xxvi.

44. *pyacle*, Latin, *piaculum*, a sin-offering, expiation.

49–50. Cf. Exodus 34. 29–30, 33: 'Moses wist not that the skin of his face shone while he talked with him. And when Aaron and all the children of Israel saw Moses, behold, the skin of his face shone; and they were afraid to come nigh him. . . . And till Moses had done speaking with them, he put a vail on his face.'

51–52. *Josue . . . that heng the kynges of Gabaoon.* Cf. Joshua 10. 16, 22, 26: 'But these five kings fled, and hid themselves in a cave at Makkedah. . . . Then said Joshua, Open the mouth of the cave, and bring out those five kings unto me out of the cave. . . . And afterward Joshua smote them, and slew them, and hanged them on five trees: and they were hanging upon the trees until the evening.'

53. *Nor the noble myghty Gedeoon.* Cf. Judges 6. 12: 'And the angel of the Lord appeared unto him, and said unto him, The Lord is with thee, thou mighty man of valour.'

57. *Sampson that rent the lion | On pecis smalle.* Cf. Judges 14. 5–6: 'Then went Samson down, and his father and his mother, to Timnath, and came to the vineyards of Timnath; and, behold, a young lion roared

against him. And the spirit of the Lord came mightily upon him, and he rent him as he would a kid, and he had nothing in his hand.'

60. Cf. I Samuel 17. No Bible story was more popular in the Middle Ages, if we may judge by the constant references to it which we find. It formed the three lections of the first nocturn of the fourth Sunday after Pentecost, and was continued in the lections of Monday and Tuesday. It also formed the subject of one of St. Augustine's popular sermons (cf. Professor Manly's article, *Familia Goliae*, in Mod. Phil. Oct. 1907); and it is constantly referred to in the sacred Latin hymns published by Dreves.

65 ff. Cf. Rev. 6. 8: 'And I looked, and behold a pale horse: and his name that sat on him was Death, and Hell followed with him. And power was given unto them over the fourth part of the earth, to kill with the sword, and with hunger, and with death, and with the beasts of the earth.'

39

Printed, Wright, *Rel. Antiq.* I, 57. Other metrical versions of the Lord's Prayer are: (1) MS. Gg. IV, 32. Bib. Cantab.; printed Wright, *Rel. Antiq.* I, 159. (2) MS. Hh. VI, 11, Cambridge Pub. Lib.; printed. *ibid.* 169. (3) MS. Arundel, 292, fol. 3; printed, *ibid.* 235. (4) MS, Cotton. Cleopatra, B. vi. fol. 201; printed, *ibid.* 22; also Maskell, II, 238. (5) The Makculloch MS. f. 87 a; described, Gregory Smith, *Spec. of Middle Scots*, p. lxviii.

40

Printed, Clark, E. E. T. S. 129–5.

6. *Iff we make clene oure tempil with-ynne.* Cf. 1 Cor. 3. 16–17: 'Know ye not that ye are the temple of God, and that the Spirit of God dwelleth in you? If any man defile the temple of God, him shall God destroy; for the temple of God is holy, which temple ye are.' Cf. also 1 Cor. 6. 19.

41

Printed, Morris, E. E. T. S. 53–258. A very free paraphrase of the Lord's prayer.

1. Cf. 3–18, note.

2. *king of alle kinge.* Liturgical.

36. *þu ert hele & help & lif & king of alle kinge.* Cf. 31–11, 12: 'þu art hele and lif and liht | And helpest al mon-kunne.'

42

Printed, Wright, *Rel. Antiq.* II, 228. See No. 11, note. This poem, by friar William Herebert, is a close translation of the hymn, *Ave Maris Stella*, used in the services of the Horae, BVM., especially as the hymn in Evensong.

25–26. The *Gloria Patri* was regularly appended to all hymns in the services; translated in the Prymer: 'Preisyng be to god the fadir, worshipe to the hiȝest crist, and to the hooli goste: oon worship to hem thre.' Mask. II, 62.

43

Printed, Furnivall, E. E. T. S. 117–735. One of the most interesting and delightful paraphrases in Middle English. The structure of the poem is worthy of notice. Two stanzas of the paraphrase are devoted to each stanza of the original. In each case the first stanza is a closer paraphrase than the second, and in each case the first line of the first stanza is a close translation, and the second line is not a translation, but a suitable expansion of the first; the third line goes back to the original, the fourth is an expansion, and so on through the eight lines. The last four lines have a different rhyme scheme, and serve as a kind of refrain. The second stanza attempts a re-paraphrasing in the same manner, except that the odd lines are usually much freer even than in the first stanza. There are many Latin hymns built upon the *Ave Maris Stella* (cf. Mone II, Nos. 496–500), but I can discover in them no signs of relationship with this poem.

20. *Out of þis wopes dale.* The liturgical *in this valei of teeris;* found in the antiphon, *Salve regina,* and very frequently in Latin hymns and sacred poetry. It is not found elsewhere in these poems. With the general thought of ll. 20–24 may be compared the following responses and versicles from the same antiphon: '*Resp.* O celi. *Vers.* Reiside aboue heuenes: and crowned of thi child in this wrecchid vale, to giltie be lady of forȝeuenes. *Resp.* O hooly. *Vers.* That he lose us fro synnes for the loue of his modir: and to the kyngdom of clernesse lede us the kyng of pitee.' Mask. II, 73.

79. With the general thought of the remainder of the stanza may be compared the antiphon, *O gloriosa:* 'O thou gloriouse modir of god, euer mayde that desseruedist to bere the lord of alle thingis: and thou mayde aloone to ȝeue souke to the king of angels.' Mask. II, 26.

93. *Ladi briht, wiþ eiȝen gray. Eiȝen gray* are of course the only kind of eyes allowed to the beloved of the *chansons d'amour;* likewise her complexion was always bright.

129. *Ladi . . . feir and fre.* This epithet, which has been repeated with great frequency by English lyric poets (cf., for example, Milton, *L'Allegro,* 'Goddess, fair and free'), was doubtless introduced into England from the French lyric poets. Cf. Bern MS. 389: 'dame, douche et franche.'

130. *þu lilye whyt of face.* Cf. the Sequence, In die Assump. B. M.: 'Purpurea ut viola, roscida ut rosa, candens ut lilia.' Surtees Soc. 60–82.

44

Printed, Wright, *Rel. Antiq.* II, 229. See Nos. 11 and 42 and the notes. A translation of the hymn, *Veni, Creator Spiritus.* Another version of this hymn is found in the Vernon MS.; printed E. E. T. S. 98–43.

45

Printed, Simmons, E. E. T. S. 71–18.

2. Liturgical; cf. 2–10, note.

4. *þo gode to chese & leeue þo ille.* Ultimately from Is. 7. 15, 16: 'refuse the evil and choose the good.' But the use of the quotation was very widespread, owing to its occurrence in patristic writings, especially in the *Mirror* of St. Edmund.

46

Printed, Dyboski, E. E. T. S. E. S. 101–51; previously, Flügel, Anglia, 26 (1906) 157. Maskell says: 'In the Salisbury Horae and Prymers is commonly found an Office to the "Proper Angel."' It has never been pointed out that this poem is a free translation of the antiphon, versicle, and response belonging to that office.

1–3. Cf. the antiphon: 'Angele qui meus es custos, pietate superna: Me tibi commissum, salva, defende, guberna.' Mask. II, 268.

9–13. Cf. 'O tu dulcis angele, qui mecum moraris, Licet personaliter mecum non loquaris. Animam cum corpore precor tuearis.'

14. A reminiscence of the litany. Cf. 5–22, note.

15. *For þat ys thyn offes.* Cf. 'Tuum hoc est officium.' *Ibid.*

16. Cf.: '*Vers.* O beate angele, nuntie Dei nostri.

      Resp. Actus meos regula ad votum Dei altissimi.' *Ibid.*

47

Printed, Furnivall, E. E. T. S. 117–756; previously in Archiv 97 (1896) 312. *A rhyme-beginning poem.* Furnivall.

18. *Haytit.* " ? for *hantith*, practises." Furnivall.

48

Printed, Furnivall, E. E. T. S. 117–744.

1 ff. This poem follows the general form for morning devotions which St. Edmund suggested in his *Speculum.* The first stanza is a free paraphrase of his *Oratio in mane.* I quote, however, the Prayer as given in a paraphrase in a treatise on *Daily Work*, printed in *R. R.* I, 145, which is nearer the form in the text: 'I thank þe, dereworthi lorde, with al mi hert: þat so vnworthi wreche þus has ȝemid þis night, & tholid me with life & hele þus abide þis daie (ll. 3–4). I thanke þe, lorde, of þis grete gode & mani oþer,' etc. St. Edmund concludes: 'et pro alijs vniuersis bene-

ficijs tuis que michi tua sola pietate contulisti, qui viuis & regnas deus &
. . . Dere frende in þis same manere sall þou say when þou rysez at morne
and when þou lygges down at evyn.' *Mirror*, E. E. T. S. 26ᵃ-19.

15. *I be-take þis day of me cure.* Also: *My body and soule I þe be-take,*
l. 19. Cf. St. Edmund: 'And, dere frende, do na thynge in þis lfye till
þou commend þi selfe . . . in the handis of thi swete Lorde Ihesu Criste,
and say one þis manere, In manus tuas, Domine . . . commendo in hac
nocte (vel die) animam meam et corpus meum.' *Ibid.*

20. *þis day, lord, kep me out of synne.* Cf.: 'custodi nos, Domine,
in hac nocte (vel die) . . . a peccatis.' *Ibid.*

23-24. *ffrom þi lawe þat I ne twynne | ne breke þi ten commaundements.*
Cf.: 'et fac me semper tuis obedire mandatis, & a te numquam separari
permittas.' *Ibid.*

25 ff. Cf. St. Edmund: 'Now, dere frende, be-fore matyns sall þou
thynke of þe swete byrthe of Ihesu Cryste alþer-fyrste, and sythyn eftyr-
warde of his passion.' *Ibid.* 40.

27-32. Cf. *Oratio*, translated: 'kepe vs, Lorde, in þis nyghte (or þis
day) . . . fra vices and fra wykked ȝernynges, fra synns and . . . fra
þe paynes of helle.' *Ibid.* 20.

33-36. Cf. St. Edmund *supra;* also: 'Be-fore pryme, þou sall thynke
of þe passion of Ihesu . . . and þay bygan to dryfe hym till hethynge,
and to fulle hym als a fule, and spite one hym in dispyte in his faire face;
. . . and sythen asked hym whate he was þat hym smate.' *Ibid*, 41.

41-44. Cf.: 'Of his passyon, sall þou thynke how þe Iewes ledde hym
in-to þaire counsaile, and bare false wytnes agayne hym, and put appone
hym þat . . . he had said þat he suld haue distroyde þe temple of Godde,
and make agayne anoþer with-in the thirde day.' *Ibid.*

63-64. Patristic phrases much used by mystic writers.

67-68. From the Confession; cf. 2, note.

49

Printed, Horstmann, E. E. T. S. 98-26. It has never been pointed out
that this poem is a rendering of a prayer by St. Thomas of Aquinas.
Prose translations of this prayer are frequent. Queen Mary translated
it into good English prose in 'the xi yere of here age' (Mask. II, 266).
The original Latin follows: —

'*Oratio solita recitari singulo die ante imaginem Christi.*

'Concede mihi, misericors Deus, quae tibi placita sunt ardenter con-
cupiscere, prudenter investigare, veraciter agnoscere, et perfecte adim-
plere ad laudem et gloriam nominis tui. Ordina statum meum, et quod
a me requiris ut faciam, tribue ut sciam; et da exequi sicut oportet et
expedit animae meae. Da mihi, Domine Deus meus, inter prospera et
adversa non deficere, ut in illis non extollar, et in istis non deprimar:

de nullo gaudeam vel doleam nisi quod ducat ad te vel abducat a te.
Nulli placere appetam, vel displicere timeam nisi tibi. Vilescant mihi,
Domine, omnia transitoria, et cara mihi sint omnia tua. Taedeat me
gaudii quod est sine te, nec aliud cupiam quod est extra te. Delectet me,
Domine, labor qui est pro te; et taediosa sit mihi omnis quies quae est
sine te. Frequenter da mihi, Domine, cor ad te dirigere, et in defectione
mea cum emendationis proposito dolendo pensare. Fac me, Domine
Deus, obedientem sine contradictione, pauperem sine defectione, castum
sine corruptione, patientem sine murmuratione, humilem sine fictione,
et hilarem sine dissolutione, tristem sine dejectione, maturum sine
gravitate, agilem sine levitate, timentem te sine desperatione, veracem
sine duplicitate, operantem bona sine praesumptione, proximum cor-
ripere sine elatione, ipsum aedificare verbo et exemplo sine simulatione.
Da mihi, Domine Deus, cor pervigil quod nulla abducat a te curiosa
cogitatio. Da nobile quod nulla deorsum trahat indigna affectio. Da
rectum nulla seorsum obliquet sinistra intentio. Da firmum quod nulla
frangat tribulatio. Da liberum quod nulla sibi vindicet violenta affectio.
Largire mihi, Domine Deus meus, intellectum te cognoscentem, diligentiam
te quaerentem, sapientiam te invenientem, conversationem tibi placentem,
perseverantiam fidenter te expectantem, et fiduciam te finaliter am-
plectentem: tuis poenis hic affligi per poenitentiam, tuis beneficiis in via
uti per gratiam, tuis gaudiis in primis in patria perfrui per gloriam.
Qui vivis et regnas Deus per omnia saecula saeculorum. Amen.'

Thomae Aquinatis . . . *Opera omnia*, Vol. XXXII, 820.

50

Printed, Furnivall, E. E. T. S. 117–733.

1. *In Somer bi-fore þe Ascenciun; i.e.* some time in May or early June,
Ascension coming the fortieth day after Easter.

4. *ffor þe þees fast gon I prai.* 'For the pees' is the name of a collect
used in Evensong. It was evidently so named from its chief petition:
'Deus a quo sancta desideria, recta consilia, et justa sunt opera: da
servis tuis illam quam mundus dare non potest pacem.' Mask. II, 36.

8. *Mane nobiscum, Domine,* formed the versicle for the fourth Sunday
after Easter. This may be the Sunday to which the poet refers.

11. *In Concience and we be clene | Digne þi, lorde, with vs to dwelle.*
Cf. 'Mentis nostrae sordes ablue, ut in nobis manere tu digneris.' MS.
Bod. 775. Surtees Soc. 60–250.

17–24. Cf. Luke 24. 13 ff.: 'Et ecce duo ex illis ibant ipsa die in
castellum quod erat in spatio stadiorum sexaginta ab Jerusalem, nomine
Emmaus. . . . Et factum est, dum fabularentur et secum quaererunt,
et ipse Jesus appropinquans ibat cum illis. . . . Et respondens unus
cui nomen Cleophas. . . . Appropinquaverunt castello, quo ibant et

ipse se finxit longius ire.   Et coegerunt illum dicentes: Mane nobiscum,
quoniam advesperascit et inclinata est jam dies.   Et intravit cum illis.'
　75–76. Liturgical.
　77. From the Confession.

51.

Printed, Horstmann, E. E. T. S. 98–34.
　2. *þe seuen ȝiftes of þe holigost.*   Cf. 3–73, note.

52

Printed, Furnivall, E. E. T. S. 24–15; Wülcker, *Alteng. Lesebuch,*
2–5.   The popularity of this poem in the fifteenth century is evidenced
by its many variants; I have noted the following; there are doubtless
others:
　(*A*) Lambeth MS. 853; printed here.
　(*B*) Stonyhurst College MS. B. XLIII, ff. 96^b–97^b; printed, Hulme,
E. E. T. S. E. S. 100–xxxviii; eight stanzas of fours, and as usual sadly
disarranged.
　(*C*) Vernon MS.; printed, Horstmann, E. E. T. S. 98–48; eight
stanzas of fours, badly arranged.
　(*D*) MS. of the Marquis of Bath; unpublished; described, *Hist.
MSS. Com.* III, 180.
　(*E*) MS. of Lord Leconfield; unpublished; described, *Hist. MSS.
Com.* VI, 289.
　(*F*) MS. Trinity Coll. Camb. $\left\{{B. 14. 19 \atop 483}\right.$ fol. 162 b; unpublished; described, James, *Western MSS.* I, 419.
　(*G*) MS. Cotton. Vesp. A **XXV**; printed, Lemcke's *Jahrbuch, Neue
Folge,* III, 111.
　1–2. Liturgical; cf. 2–4, note.   The idea is very common in mystic
treatises; cf. *R. R.* I, 70: 'Lufe Ihesu, for he made þe, and boght þe ful
dere.'
　5. [*is*].   Furnivall prints 'in.'
　11. Several lines in this poem seem to be reminiscent of the Prayer
of St. Thomas of Aquinas, a form of which is printed as No. 49.   Cf.
with this line: 'Fac me, Domine Deus . . . humilem sine fictione.'
　21. *Ihesu, graunte me myne askinge,* | *Perfite pacience in my disese.*
Cf. 'Da mihi, Domine Deus meus inter . . . adversa non deficere;'
translated in No. 49: 'And euere beo pacient in wo.'
　23–24. *And neuere mote y do þat þing* | *þat schulde þee in ony wise dis-
plese.*   Cf.: 'Nulli placere appetam, vel displicere timeam nisi tibi.'
　43. *And sende hemfruytis of erþeli fode* | *As ech man nediþ in his degree.*
Cf. the Litany: 'That thou fouche saaf to ȝyue and kepe the fruytis of
the erthe: we preien thee to heere us.'   Mask. II, 104.

49. *Ihesu, þat art þe goostli stoon | Of al holi chirche in myddil erþe.*
Cf. Matt. 21. 42 :‘Jesus saith unto them, Did ye never read in the
scriptures, The stone which the builders rejected, the same is become the
head of the corner.' Also 1 Peter 2. 6 : 'Wherefore also it is contained
in the scripture, Behold, I lay in Sion a chief corner stone, elect, precious :
and he that believeth on him shall not be confounded.'

51. *Bringe þi fooldis & flockis in oon, | And rule hem riȝtli with oon hirde.*
Cf. John 10. 16 : 'And other sheep I have, which are not of this fold :
them also I must bring, and they shall hear my voice; and there shall
be one fold, and one shepherd.'

53

Printed, Perry, E. E. T. S. 26ᵃ–73; also Horstman, *R. R.* I, 364.
'R. Rolle's authorship is beyond doubt.' (Horstman.) Some of the
lines in this poem occur also in poems in the mystic tract, *Ego dormio et
cor meum vigilat.* Horstman called attention to two parallel stanzas,
to which I add other lines. This poem and the following show the influence of mystic thought and writings in almost every line; there is no
need to seek for obvious parallels in mystic treatises. No. 53 consists in
reality of two lyrics — the first, extending to l. 40, is a pure penitential
lyric; the second, from l. 40, is a song of love-longing.

9. *Iesu Criste, Goddes sone of heuen.* A phrase often used in patristic
writings.

17. *Iesu of whaym all gudnes sprynges.* Cf. Oratio, Inhumatio De-
functi : 'Deus . . . de cujus munere venit omne quod bonum est, et
procedet.' Mask. I, 127.

38–40. Cf. *Ego dormio:* 'þow make me clene of synne, & lat vs neuer
twyn; kyndel me fire with-in, þat I þi lufe may wyn.' *R. R.* I, 57.

41–42. Cf. *R. R.* I, 58 : 'þe I couete, þis world noght, & for it I fle;
þou ert þat I haue soght : þi face when may I see ?'

45, 47. Cf. *R. R.* I, 57 : 'Ihesu . . . þi lufe in to me send, þat I may
with þe lend.'

46, 48. Cf. *R. R.* I, 60 : 'in til þi lyght me lede, and in thi lufe me
fede : In lufe make me to spede, þat þou be euer my mede.'

65–67. Cf. *R. R.* I, 60 : 'Ihesu my dere & my drewry, delyte ert þou
to syng : Ihesu my myrth & melody, when will þow com my keyng ?'
(Horstman.)

68. Cf. *R. R.* I, 57 : 'Ihesu, receyu my hert, & to þi lufe me bryng.'

69–70. Cf. *R. R.* I, 60 : 'Ihesu, my hele & my hony, my whart & my
comfortyng : Ihesu, I couayte for to dy, when it es þi payng.'

71–72. Cf. *R. R.* I, 61 : 'for lufe my bale may bete | And til hys blis
me brynge.'

73–76. Cf. *R. R.* I, 57 : 'In lufe þow wownde my thoght, and lyft
my hert to þe : my sawle þou dere hase boght, þi lufer make it to be.'
(Horstman.)

54

Printed, Furnivall, E. E. T. S. 15 –139.

55

Printed, Horstmann, E. E. T. S. 98–131.

56

Printed, Horstmann, E. E. T. S. 98–22. The two stanzas of this poem are usually found separately. Variants of stanza 1 are: (1) MS. Harl. 2316, fol. 25, r°; printed, Wright, *Rel. Antiq.* II, 119. (2) Vernon MS. fol. CCXCIX, as the last stanza (32) of a long poem, *A Mournyng Song of thi loue of God;* printed, Furnivall, E. E. T. S. 117–476. (3) MS. of Lord Mostyn, No. 186. This variant is so interesting that I print it here. It is found in a MS. of a Latin *Horae ad usum Ecclesiae Romae,* about the middle of the volume:

> Ladye mary mayden swete
> that art so good and fayre and fre
> Wyth al myn herte I the beseeche
> for thi joyes to i thre.
> That also faste into myn herte
> mote thy love takyn be
> As was the sorwe in thyn herte
> tho yi leue sone duyed for me.
>
> *Hist. MSS. Com.* IV, 355.

Variant of stanza 2, MS. Thornton, fol. 191ᵇ; printed, Horstman, *R. R.* I, 364. For an appreciation of the metrical skill shown in this poem, see Saintsbury, *Hist. of Eng. Pros.* I, 130.

57

Printed, Clarke, E. E. T. S. 129–4.

2. *And kepe vs from perel of synnes and payne.* Cf. the Litany: 'Fro dredeful pereles of oure synnes: lord delyuer us.' Mask II, 101.

10. Liturgical; cf. 3–10, note.

12–13. Probably an echo from St. Edmund; cf. the *Mirror,* especially the following passage: 'here, I say, es takyn of gret lufe, þat he deyned hym to make vs till his awen lyknes righte als we had bene his awen chosen childyre . . . he moghte hafe made vs at his will anykyn oþer bestis, and þan had we dyede to-gedire bathe body and saule. Bot when he hade made vs man . . . now es na herte sa harde þat it na moghte nesche and lufe swylke a Godde with all his myghte.' E. E. T. S. 26ᵃ–31.

25. This petition from the Lord's prayer was often used; it occurs in

a response in the Horae, BVM. : ' *Versus*. And lede us not in to tempta-
cioun. *Resp*. But delyuer us fro yuel.' Mask. II, 10. Cf. also the
Litany: 'Ab omni malo, libera nos, domine.'

58

Printed, Zupitza, Eng. Stud. 11 (1887) 423. For a careful study of
the variant MSS. of St. Godric's songs, see the same. The poems are
printed, Ritson, *Bibliog. Poet*. 1–4; Stevenson, *Libellus de vita et miraculis S. Godrici*, 288 (only one stanza of 59); and elsewhere. There are
three English songs by the Saint, preserved in various lives. The anonymous legend in the Harleian MS. contains an interesting account: 'Die
quadam raptus in exstasim, ab hora diei prima usque ad nonam palmas
in coelum tenebat erectas, lacrimisque fluentibus invocabat Dei piissi-
mam Genitricem, quasi praesentialiter assistentem. Saepe psallebat,
frequenter orabat. Canticum plerumque dulcissimum decantabat, in
cujus fine sic flebat, ut illud repetere non valebat. Illud a beatissima
Dei Genitrice didicerat, sicut mihi postea secretius indicavit. Interim
oravit hoc modo.' Here follows the Latin of the first stanza of 59, then
the English with musical notation. Ritson remarks in a note: 'By
the assistance of the Latin versions one is enabled to give it literally
in English, as follows: Saint Mary, chaste virgin, mother of Jesus Christ
of Nazareth, take, shield, help, thy Godric; take, bring him quickly with
thee into God's kingdom. Saint Mary, Christ's chamber, purity of
a maiden, flower of a mother, destroy my sin, reign in my mind, bring
me to dwell with the only God.' More exhaustive comment is omitted
since the poem has already been thoroughly investigated.

59

Printed, Wright, *Rel. Antiq*. II, 120. These ejaculatory verses to
Mary seem to have been well known. A variant is found as an inlaid
stanza to Mary in the Vernon MS. of the long poem on the passion of
Jesus, beginning, *Swete Ihesu, now wol I synge;* printed, Horstman, *R. R.*
II, 14; Furnivall, E. E. T. S. 117–454.

60

Hitherto unprinted. Perhaps the most popular of the later poems to
Mary. It occurs in the *Speculum Christiani*, printed by Machlinia, c.
1485. The poem is sometimes ascribed to John Watton, but it was
doubtless a popular poem before being incorporated in the *Speculum*.
Variants are: (*A*) Harl. MS. 2382; printed here. (*B*) Camb. Pub. Lib.
MS. Ff. v. 48; printed, Wright, *Rel. Antiq*. II, 212. (*C*) Chetam Lib.
MS. 8009. f. 121^a-4-121^{b}u; unprinted; described, Kölbing, Eng. Stud.
7 (1884) 197. (*D*) Brit. Mus. MS. C. 11. a. 28, p. 97 (Speculum Xristiani);

printed Dibdin, *Typ. Antiq.* II, 13; also (first 20 ll.), Flügel, *Neueng. Lesebuch*, p. 10.

This prayer to Mary shows no influence of the *chanson d'amour*, but seems rather to belong to the more commonplace poetry that succeeded the *chansons* in the fifteenth century in France. The stylistic trick of *Anaphora*, so prominent in this poem, was very popular in French poetry of the time. Though this poem in its general origin owes much to late French poetry, there can be little doubt that in this instance the anaphora has been ultimately influenced chiefly by the Litany, and this fact in turn suggests that perhaps the constant use of the Litany in the Middle Ages has much to do with the widespread popularity of this mannerism. The parallels between this poem and the Litany are not strikingly close in their phrases; such passages as the following show, however, the similiarity of ideas, development, and wording: 'Fro al yuel: lord, delyuer us. (Cf. l. 6.) Fro the aweitingis of the fend: lord, delyuer us (l. 22). Fro endeles dampnacioun: lord, delyuer us (l. 16). Fro dredeful pereles of oure synnes: lord delyuer us. Fro feere of the enemy: lord, delyuer us. Fro unclene thouȝtis: lord, delyuer us. . . . That thou yelde euerlastynge goodis to oure good doeris: we prein. . . . That thou fouche saaf to ȝyue and kepe the fruytis of the erthe: we preien thee to heere us.' Mask. II, 101.

1. Liturgical; cf. 30-1, note.
14. [*mine*]. MS. has *me*.
20. *fame*. The word *name* has been crossed out before *fame*.
43. A second *me* precedes *haue* in MS.
49. A paraphrase of the Salutation.
51. *flour of al þi kny.* Cf. the Horae, BVM., Ant.: 'flour of virgyns.' Mask. II, 75.

61

Printed, Hortsmann, E. E. T. S. 98-22. The popularity of No. 60 is shown as much by its influence upon succeeding lyrics as by the large number of MS. copies extant of the poem itself. The present poem is little more than a variant of No. 60, but because of the unique way in which it is expanded I have printed it here, where it may be compared with its original line by line. The poem in its expanded form is quite as free from the manner of the chanson as it was in its earlier form.

62

Printed, Horstmann, E. E. T. S. 98-33. Shows the influence of No. 60 in rhyme couplets, in phrases, in petitions for protection, and in general method of development; the resemblance in phraseology, however, is not striking. The liturgical sources for the epithets for Mary, and other expressions, since they have been pointed out in detail previously, need no repetition here.

1. *Mary modur.* Cf. 69–1 : 'Mary moder.'

2. *þenk on me.* Cf. 60–2 : 'thenk on me.'

10. *And let me neuere die þer-Inne.* Cf. 60–36 : 'lat hem neuere dye ther ynne.'

17–19. Cf. 60, 21–24.

25. *Marie, Mi ffrendes, quike and dede,* etc. Cf. 60–27 : 'And for my friends y pray the,' *etc.*

63

Printed, Horstmann, E. E. T. S. 98–133. Like the previous poem, this lyric is also reminiscent of No. 60.

1–2. Cf. 60, 1–2.

3. Cf. 60–21.

6. *þat me ne dere no wiht.* Also ll. 35–36. Cf. 60–23.

11. *As þou art flour of alle.* Cf. 60–51.

13. Cf. 61, 3–4.

14. It has never been noticed in this connection that the five joys of the Virgin formed a portion of the devotions of the Horae, BVM. Though the idea was ultimately patristic without doubt, it was from liturgical sources that the English poets received their inspiration to sing the joys of Mary. I subjoin the rendering in the Prymer :

'An othir salutacioun to oure lady. Gaude virgo mater

'Heil thou, virgyne modir of crist, that bi eere conceyuedist : thurȝ gabriels message.

'Heil thou, for ful with god, childedist withoute peyne : with lilye of chastite.

'Heil thou, for of thi sone whom thou sorwedist to suffre deeth : the resurrexioun shyneth.

'Heil thou, crist up stiȝynge, and in to heuene thee seynge : is born bi his owne mouyng.

'Heil marie, that after him stiȝest, and it is to thee greet honoure : in the palece of heuene.

'Where the fruyt of thi wombe, bi thee is ȝouun us to use : in euerlast-ynge ioye. Amen.' Mask. II, 73.

64

Printed, Morris, E. E. T. S. 53–257.

65

Printed, Morris, E. E. T. S. 49–195; previously, Wright, *Rel. Antiq.* I, 102; Mätzner, 54; Böddeker, 457. Variant, Harl. MS. 2253, fol. 80; printed, Wright, *Spec. of L. P.*, p. 93; Böddeker, 216.

1. A paraphrase of the salutation.

2. *Moder of milde[r]tnisse.* Cf. the antiphon, Horae, BVM.: 'Heil, queene, modir of merci.' Mask. II, 71.

29. *Bricht and scene quen of storre, so me liht and lere, | In this false fikele world so me led and steore.* This thought, that Mary should guide the wanderer in this world as a star guides the mariner, and thence, probably, that Christ should also direct the way (cf. l. 4), was extremely popular in medieval religious poetry, and was doubtless a development from the hymn, *Ave Maris Stella*, which was in daily use in the services. Cf. 69–22, note.

66

Printed, Chambers and Sidgwick, p. 89.

21–22. Cf. 25–39, note.

32–33. *Monkun wid thi bodi abouht, | Thou noldest lesen hym for nouht.* Cf. the versicle after the ninth lesson in the Offices of the Dead: 'Now, crist, we axen thee haue merci, we bisechen thee, thou that camest to bigge that weren born: wile thou not dampne hem that thou hast bouȝt.' Mask. II, 146.

67

Printed, Horstmann, E. E. T. S. 98–30. Variant, only 29 ll. and inferior in arrangement, Lambeth MS. 853, fol. 26; printed, Furnivall, E. E. T. S. 24–6. This poem and the following are poetical paraphrases of the liturgical salutation of the five joys of the Virgin, a form of which is printed in the note to 63–14. It is unnecessary to point out the closeness of the parallels.

11. *And þou were Maid biforn: And aftur, as we rede.* Cf. the York Manual, *In die Paschae*, Antiphona: 'Virgo prius ac posterius.' Surtees Soc. 63–18*.

33. *Ladi seinte Marie: So Rose in Erber rede.* A theme often celebrated. A Frenchman in the 14th century wrote a book on 'la vision de la Rose' in which he explained that 'la glorieuse Vierge Marie est comparée à la rose pour ses proprietes.' The prologue was entitled: 'Quasi plantio rose in Iherico. Ecclesiatici xxiiii.' The author of the *Mirroure of oure Ladye* similarly declares: 'Therefore she ys moste worthy lykened to a rose. and veryly to a rose in iherico. for as men redeth. that a rose of that place passeth in hys fayrenes other flowers.' E. E. T. S. E. S. 19–243.

68

Printed, Morris, E. E. T. S. 49–87.

11. *Of þe ibore wiþ-ve wo.* This thought may be traced back to the early Fathers. It was used by St. Bernard in *serm.* 4, 3, *In vig. nat.*: 'conceptus fuit sine pudore, partus sine dolore.' It is found also in the Blickling Homilies (A.D. 979): 'Maria cende þonne Drihten on blisse.'

E. E. T. S. 58–3. It was ultimately taken into the liturgy, appearing in the Salutation, *Gaude virgo mater*, whence probably it was derived by the English poet. Cf. the translation, printed above: 'Heil thou, for ful with god, childedist withoute peyne: with lilye of chastite.'

12. *þat scop þe and alle þing.* Cf. the Capitulum, *Beata es*, in the *Euensong of our ladi*, Horae, BVM.: 'Blessid art thou virgyn marie, that hast born the lord maker of the world: thou hast getyn hym that made thee.' Mask. II, 61.

33–40. The poems to Mary are frequently reminiscent of the legends that are connected with her life. With these lines may be compared the following from a version of the Assumption legend; Christ is speaking to Mary: 'Moder, blith now loke þou be | And of no.thing haue þou drede. | For with mi-self I sall þe lede; | Whare I am king, þou sall be quene, | With more blis þan men may mene. . . .' | And hastili when scho come þare, | Al þe saintes þat þar ware | Honord hir halely bidene, | And þare þan was scho corond que[ne].' Horstmann, *Alt. Eng. Leg.* p. 116.

69

Printed, Furnivall, E. E. T. S. 15ᵃ–291. No poem in this collection shows more certainly the influence of the French religious lyric. The choice of epithets, the love for the French order of phrase construction in placing the noun before the adjective (*Turtill trew, Aurora bryght, Lyle fragrant, Aungels alle*, etc.), and the tendency to select rhyming words like *excellence* and *ascence*, somewhat in the manner of the *aureate style*, place this poem not only in the school of Chaucer and Lydgate, but also suggest that all these later poets when writing hymns to the Virgin went to the French religious lyric for their inspiration. To be grouped here are the following:

Chaucer's A B C poem.
Occleve's Ad beatam Virginem (2 poems).
Lgdyate's various poems to the Virgin.
Dunbar's Ane Ballot of our Lady (2 poems).

2. *Turtill trew.* This epithet is not found in the English liturgy, nor in English religious lyric poetry before Chaucer. The expression was extremely popular, however, in French poetry. St. Bernard had early called attention to the parallel: 'Turturis agnoscitur castitas in quacumque aetate. Compare uno contenta est, quo amisso alterum jam non admittit.' *In Cant.* 59, 7. So eminently fitting was the comparison that it seems to have been made immediate use of in the Latin and French hymns to Mary. So in a Latin poem of the 12th century is found, doubtless, a reference to St. Bernard's text, as follows: 'Vox tua, vox turturis.' Mone II, 515. And in the *serventois*, which grew up later, there is no more popular theme. 'La turtre entens pour la vierge Marie,'

declares the poet of the 'Taille de chant royal,' the subject of whose song is the *turtre gracieuse* (Langlois, 173), and Rutebeuf sings: 'Turtre qui ses amours ne mue.'

3. *Aurora bryght, clere as the day.* Frequent in French poetry. It is derived ultimately from the liturgy; cf. l. 17, note. The epithet, I believe, is practically unknown in English poetry before Chaucer, though it is common enough in Latin poetry. As Mone remarks (II, No. 328, note) Mary is called *Aurora* because Christ is the light of the world and the Sun of Righteousness.

5. *Lyle fragrant eke of the walle.* Cf. the hymn, *Tu miro*, translated in the *Mirroure of oure Lady:* 'Thow art veryly a swete smellynge lyllye.' E. E. T. S. E. S. 19–216. The French were especially fond of comparing Mary to a lily, a parallel which they worked out in several elaborate details; thus in the *Règles de la seconde Rhetorique* is found this bit of information for would-be religious poets: 'Item, elle est comparée à la fluer de lis, pour ce que la dicte fleur porte en milieu de soy la croix, comme elle porta Jhesu Crist en ses precieux flans.' Langlois, p. 72. *of the walle* means probably *growing beside the wall*, as descriptive of the lily.

9–11. This theme is celebrated in the hymn, *In throno*, the first stanzas of which are translated in the *Mirroure of oure Lady* as follows: 'Thou holy vyrgyn syttynge in trone nexte vnto god, geuynge thyselfe a throne to hym moste plesaunte aboue all thynges. Tho aungels that are called trones prayse wyth tho aungels that ar called potestates; and the hyghe orders of aungels, that ys cherubyn & Seraphyn, prayse the togyther with hygh soundynge praysynges.' The writer of the *Mirroure* explains that 'in the four verses of thys hympne ye prayse oure lady of seuen thynges. The fyrste ys. *that* she hathe a seat in heuen aboue all creatures next vnto god.' E. E. T. S. E. S. 19–184. The idea may go back to St. Bernard; cf. hom. 2, 1: 'Nonne tuo, immo veritatis judico, illa, quae deum habuit filium, super omnes etiam choros exaltabitur angelorum? annon deum et dominum angelorum Maria suum audacter appelat filium (Luc. 2, 48)? quis hoc audeat angelorum?' Quoted by Mone (II, p. 7) on a similar passage in a Latin hymn.

17. It seemed impossible for a poet who wrote in imitation of Lydgate to refrain from a mention of 'Phebus.' The custom of comparing Mary to the sun may be traced back through French poetry to the ancient liturgies and especially to the lines: 'rosa processit sicut sol. Oritur, ut lucifer inter astra. Velut sol micans cuncta conscendisti globorum luminaria.' Sequence, De Assump. B. M., Surtees Soc. 60–294. Cf. l. 3, note.

19. *Lady saunzpere.* A constant epithet in French poetry.

20. *Empres of helle.* A very frequent epithet in later religious poetry, both French and English. Cf. also an 'orisoun' in the Prymer: 'Heil

. . . Marie, queene of heuene; lady of the world: *empresse of helle.*'
Mask. II, 78.

22. *Stormys ayene of cruell syn | That puyssauntlye us do assayle.* St.
Bernard seems to have been the ultimate source of this very popular
thought. In the second homily on the *Missus est,* after explaining how
Mary's name means *Star of the Sea,* and how she is raised above 'this
great and spacious sea of life,' he goes on to urge: 'Whosoever thou art
who knowest thyself to be tossed about among the storms and tempests
of this troubled world rather than to be walking peacefully upon shore,
turn not thine eyes away from the shining of this star, if thou wouldst not
be overwhelmed with the tempest. If the winds of temptation arise,
if you are driving upon the rocks of tribulation, look to the star, Mary.
If you are tossed on the waves of pride, of ambition, envy, rivalry, look
to the star, invoke Mary. If wrath, avarice, temptations of the flesh
assail the frail skiff of your mind, look to Mary.' Trans. by Eales (III,
315). After St. Bernard the idea became popular in Latin, French, and
English religious writings; so that the author of the *Mirroure of oure
Ladye* declared on good authority: 'And furthermore som say that for
at matyns tyme ther apperyth a sterre in the fyrmament wherby shypmen
ar rewlyd in the see, & brynge themselfe to right hauen, & for our mercy-
full lady is that ster that socoureth mankynde in the troubelous se of this
worlde & bringeth her louers to the hauen of helth.' E. E. T. S. E. S.
19–14.

27. *Entrete þi babe, so, quene on hie, | In whom to þe is no denye.* Quite
possibly an echo from some Mary legend; cf. the following: '"Whatte-
euere it be ȝe preyon fore, | Moder," he sayth, "and quene I-core, | I
graunte wel ȝoure bone."' Horstmann, *Alt. L.* CXVI.

BIBLIOGRAPHY

I. PRINTED SOURCES OF THE MEDIEVAL ENGLISH LYRIC

This list of the printed collections of the Middle English Lyric is not
complete; only the more important are here mentioned.

BÖDDEKER, K. *Altenglische Dichtungen des MS. Harl.* 2253. Berlin,
1878.

BÖDDEKER, K. *Englische Lieder und Balladen aus dem 16. Jahrhundert.* In Lemcke's Jahrbuch, Neue Folge, ii, 81–105; 210–239;
347–367; iii, 92–129. MS. Cotton. Vesp. A. 25.

CHAMBERS, E. K., and SIDGWICK, F. *Early English Lyrics, Amorous,
Divine, Moral and Trivial.* London, 1907.

FEHR, BERNHARD. *Die Lieder der Hs. Add. 5665.* Archiv 106 (1901),
262–285.

FEHR, BERNHARD. *Die Lieder des Fairfax MS.* (Add. 5465 Brit. Mus.) Archiv 106 (1901), 48–70.

FEHR, BERNHARD. *Weitere Beiträge zur englischen Lyrik des 15. und 16. Jahrhunderts.* Archiv 107 (1901), 48–61. MSS. Sloane 2593, 1212, 3501; Harley 541, 367, 7578.

FLÜGEL, EWALD. *Liedersammlungen des xvi. Jahrhunderts, besonders aus der zeit Heinrichs VIII.* Anglia 12 (1889), 225–272; 585–597; 26 (1903), 94–285. MSS. Add. 31922; Royal MS. Appendix 58; Douce Fragments 94", 94; Bassus; Balliol 354.

FÜLGEL, EWALD. *Neuenglisches Lesebuch.* Band I, Halle, 1895.

FURNIVALL, F. J. *Early English Poems and Lives of Saints.* Transactions of the Philological Society, 1858, part ii. MSS. Harl. 913, Egerton 613, Add. 22283. Berlin, 1862.

FURNIVALL, F. J. *Hymns to the Virgin and Christ.* E. E. T. S. (1867). Chiefly from Lambeth MS. 853.

FURNIVALL, F. J. *Minor Poems of the Vernon Manuscript.* Part II. E. E. T. S. 117 (1901).

FURNIVALL, F. J. *Political, Religious, and Love Poems, from Lambeth 306 and other sources.* E. E. T. S. 15 (1866).

HALL, JOSEPH. *Short Pieces from MS. Cotton. Galba E. IX.* Eng. Stud. 21 (1895), 201–209.

HEUSER, W. *Die Kildare-Gedichte, die ältesten mittelenglischen denkmäler in Anglo-Irischen überlieferung.* Bonner Beiträge zur Anglistik, xiv (1904). Harl. MS. 913.

HORSTMANN, CARL. *The Minor Poems of the Vernon MS.* E. E. T. S. 98 (Part I, 1892).

JORDAN, R. *Kleinere Dichtungen der Handschrift Harley 3810.* Eng. Stud. 41 (1909), 253–266.

KAIL, J. *Twenty-six Political and other Poems . . . from the Oxford MSS., Digby 102 and Douce 322.* Part I, E. E. T. S. 124 (1904).

MÄTZNER, E. *Altenglische Sprachproben,* Pt. I. Berlin, 1867.

MORRIS, R. *An Old English Miscellany.* E. E. T. S. 49 (1872). Texts from Jesus College, Oxford, I, 29, Cotton. Calig. A. ix, Egerton 613, Add. 27909, etc.

MORRIS, R. *Old English Homilies of the Twelfth Century. . . . Second series, with three thirteenth century hymns from MS. 54 D. 4. 14 in Corpus Christi College, Oxford.* E. E. T. S. 53 (1873).

PADELFORD, F. M. *Early Sixteenth Century Lyrics.* Boston, 1907.

PERRY, G. G. *Religious Pieces in Prose and Verse, edited from Robert Thornton's MS. (Cir. 1440) in the Lincoln Cathedral Library.* E. E. T. S. 26 (1867).

REED, EDWARD B. *The Sixteenth Century Lyrics in Add. MS. 18752.* Anglia 33 (1910), 344–369.

ROOT, ROBERT K. *Poems from the Garrett MS.* Eng. Stud. 41 (1910), 360–379.

SMITH, G. GREGORY. *Specimens of Middle Scots.* Edinburgh, 1902.

TURNBULL, W. B. D. D. *The Visions of Tundale: together with Metrical Moralizations and other fragments of early poetry, hitherto inedited.* Edinburgh, 1843.

VARNHAGEN, HERMANN. *Die Kleinere Gedichte der Vernon-und-Simeon-Handschrift.* Anglia 7 (1884), 280–315.

WRIGHT, THOMAS. *The Owl and the Nightingale: An early English Poem attributed to Nicholas de Guildford, with some shorter poems from the same manuscript.* Percy Society 1843. Texts from MS. Cotton. Calig. A. IX.

WRIGHT, THOMAS. *Songs and Carols, now first printed from a Manuscript of the Fifteenth Century.* Percy Society 23 (1847).

WRIGHT, THOMAS. *Specimens of Old Christmas Carols.* Percy Society (1841). Texts from Sloane 2593, Harl. 2252, 5396.

WRIGHT–HALLIWELL. *Reliquiae Antiquae. Scraps from ancient Manuscripts illustrating chiefly Early English Literature and the English Language.* London, 1845.

ZUPITZA, J. *Die Gedichte der Franziskaners Jacob Ryman.* Archiv 89 (1892), 167–338.

II. CRITICAL AND OTHER WORKS

Anglia; Zeitschrift für englische Philologie enthaltend Beiträge zur Geschichte der englischen Sprache und Literatur. Halle a. S., 1877 ff.

Archiv für das Studium der neueren Sprachen und Literaturen. Begrundet von Ludwig Herrig. Braunschweig, 1846 ff.

AUST, JULIUS. *Beiträge zur Geschite der mittelenglischen Lyrik.* Archiv 70 (1883), 253–290.

BALE, JOHN. *Scriptorum illustrium majoris Britanniae Catalogus.* Basel, 1559.

— BECKER, HEINRICH. *Die Auffassung der Jungfrau Maria in der altfranzösischen litteratur.* Göttingen, 1905.

BRAKELMANN, JULIUS. *Die altfranzösische Liederhandschrift Nro. 389 der Stadtbibliothek zu Bern.* Archiv 42 (1868), 241–392; 43, 241–394.

Catalogue of the Harleian Manuscripts in the British Museum, A. London, 1808.

Catalogue Général des manuscripts des Bibliothèques Publiques de France. Paris, 1886 ff.

CHEVALIER, U. *Poésie liturgique du moyen âge.* Paris, 1893.

CHEVALIER, U. *Repertorium Hymnologicum:* catalogue des chants hymnes . . . en usage dans L'Église Latine. 2 vols. Louvain, 1892–97.

COHEN, HELEN L. *The Ballade.* This study will be a history of this type of lyric from the Middle Ages to the present time. In preparation.

DANIEL, H. A. *Thesaurus Hymnologicus Sive Hymnorum Canticorum Sequentiarum circa Annum M.D. usitatarum Collectio amplissima.* Lipsiae, 1862.

DIBDIN, T. F. *Typographical Antiquities. . . . Begun by the late Joseph Ames . . . considerably augmented by William Herbert and now greatly enlarged,* etc. 3 vols. London, 1810.

DREVES, G. M. and BLUME, C. *Analecta hymnica medii aevi.* 52 vols. Leipzig, 1886 ff.

Englischen Studien. Herausgegeben von Dr. E. Kölbing. 1877 ff.

Early English Text Society. 1864 ff.

ERSKINE, JOHN. *The Elizabethan Lyric.* New York, 1903.

GREIN UND WÜLKER. *Bibliothek der angelsächisschen Poesie.* 3 vols. Leipzig, 1883 ff.

HALLIWELL, J. O. *An Account of the European Manuscripts in the Cheltam Library, Manchester.* Manchester, 1842.

Histoire littéraire de la France. Par des Religieux bénédictins de la congrégation de S. Maur. Continuée par des membres de l'Institut. Paris, 1733 ff.

HORSTMANN, C. *Altenglische Legenden. Neue folge.* Heilbronn, 1881.

HORSTMANN, C. *Osbern Bokenam's Legenden* in Kölbing's Altenglische Bibliothek, vol. I. Heilbronn, 1883.

HORSTMAN, C. *Yorkshire Writers; Richard Rolle of Hampole and his Followers.* 2 vols. London, 1896.

INGE, WILLIAM R. *Christian Mysticism: considered in eight lectures, delivered before the University of Oxford.* London, 1899.

Jahrbuch für romanische und englische Sprache und Litteratur. Herausgegeben von Ludwig Lemcke. Neue Folge, 1874 ff.

JAMES, M. R. *A Descriptive Catalogue of the Manuscripts in the Library of Emmanuel College.* Cambridge, 1904. (All the descriptive catalogues by Mr. James should be consulted.)

JEANROY, A. *Les Origines de la Poésie lyrique en France au Moyen Age.* Deuxième edition, avec additions et un appendice bibliographique. Paris, 1904.

JEANROY, A. *Mélanges d'Ancienne Poésie Lyrique. Chansons, Jeux Partis, et Refrains Inédits du xiijᵉ Siècle.* Paris, 1902.

JUBINAL, ACHILLE. *Œuvres complètes de Rutebeuf, Trouvère du xiiie Siècle.* Paris, 1874.

LANGLOIS, E. *Recueil d'arts de seconde rhétorique.* Paris, 1902.

LAUCHERT, F. *Ueber das Englische Marienlied im 13 Jahrhundert.* Engl. Stud. 16 (1891), 124–142.

MABILLON, J. *Sancti Bernardi abbotis primi Clarae-Vallensis Opera omnia.* Parisiis, 1719.

MACAULAY, G. C. *The Complete Works of John Gower.* Oxford, 1901.

MACCRACKEN, HENRY NOBLE. *The Lydgate Canon.* Appendix to the Philological Society's Transactions, 1907–1909. London, 1908.

MARTÈNE, EDMUND. *De antiques ecclesiae ritibus ligri tres ex variis insigniorum ecclesiarum pontificalibus sacramentariis missalibus.* 4 vols. Collecti Antverpiæ, 1763–64.

MASKELL, WILLIAM. *Monumenta Ritualia Ecclesiæ Anglicanæ.* 3 vols. London, 1846–47.

MASKELL, WILLIAM. *The Ancient Liturgy of the Church of England, according to the uses of Sarum, Bangor, York and Hereford, and the Modern Roman Liturgy.* London, 1846.

MEYER, P. *Les Manuscrits Français de Cambridge.* Romania 15 (1886), 236–357.

MEYER, P. *Mélanges de Poésie Anglo-Normande.* Romania 4 (1875), 370–397.

MEYER, P. *Notice et Extraits du MS. 8336 de la Bibliothèque de Sir Thomas Phillipps à Cheltenham.* Romania 13 (1884), 497–541.

MEYER, P. *Notice du MS. Bodley 57.* Romania 35 (1906), 570–582.

MIGNE, J. P. *Patrologiae cursus completus . . . series Latina.* Parisiis, 1844–80.

Modern Language Notes. Baltimore, 1886 ff.

Modern Philology. Chicago, 1903 ff.

MONE, F. J. *Hymni Latini Medii Aevi.* 3 vols. Friburgi, 1853–55.

MOREL, P. GALL. *Lateinische Hymnen des Mittelalters.* Einsiedeln, 1866.

MURRAY, J. A. H. *A New English Dictionary on Historical Principles.* Oxford, 1888 ff.

PALGRAVE, F. T. *The Golden Treasury.* London, 1861.

PARIS, GASTON. *La Littérature Française au Moyen Age.* Paris, 1905.

PARIS, GASTON. *Les Origines de la Poésie Lyrique en France au moyen âge.* Extrait du Journal des Savants. Paris, 1892.

POLLARD, A. W. *Fifteenth Century Prose and Verse.* Westminster, 1903.

RAYNAUD, GASTON. *Bibliographie des Chansonniers Français des xiiie et xive Siècles.* Paris, 1884.

RAYNAUD, GASTON. *Recueil de Motets français des xiie et xiiie Siècles.* 2 vols. Paris, 1881–83.

Reports of the Historical Manuscripts Commission. London, 1883 ff.

RITSON, JOSEPH. *Bibliographia Poetica.* London, 1802.

Romania: Recueil Trimestriel consacré à l'étude des langues et des littératures Romanes. Paris, 1872 ff.

SCHAFF, PHILIP. *Rise and Progress of Maryolatry.* Contemporary Review, April, 1867.

SCHIPPER, J. *The Poems of William Dunbar.* Denkschriften der kaiserlichen Akademie der Wissenschaften. Vols. 40–42. Wien, 1892–93.

SCHIPPER, J. *Englische Metrik.* Bonn, 1881.

SCHIPPER, J. *A History of English Versification.* Oxford, 1910.

SIMMONS, T. F. *The Lay-Folks' Mass-Book.* E. E. T. S. 71 (1879).

Société des Anciens Textes Français. Paris, 1875 ff.

STEFFENS, GEORG. *Die altfranzösische Liedhandschrift der Bodleiana in Oxford, Douce 308.* Archiv 97 (1896), 283–308; 98 (1897), 59–80; 343–382; 99 (1897), 77–100; 339–388; 104 (1900), 331–354.

STENGEL, E. M. *Codicem manu scriptum Digby 86.* Halis, 1871.

STEVENSON, J. *Anglo-Saxon and Early English Psalter.* Surtees Soc. 1843.

STEVENSON, J. *Libellus de vita et miraculis S. Godrici.* Surtees Soc. 1847.

STOBART, J. C. *The Chaucer Epoch.* London, no date.

Surtees Society, The Publications of the. London, 1835 ff.

TEN BRINK, B. *Geschichte der Englischen Litteratur.* Berlin, 1877. Vol. I, translated by H. M. Kennedy, New York, 1889.

Thomae Aquinatis . . . Opera Omnia. Parisiis, 1879.

Three Primers Put Forth in the Reign of Henry VIII. Oxford, 1848.

THORPE, THOMAS. *Catalogue of upwards of fourteen hundred manuscripts upon vellum and paper.* London, 1836.

VOLLHARDT, W. *Einfluss der Lateinischen geistlichen Litteratur auf einige kleinere Schöpfungen der Englischen übergangsperiode.* Leipzig, 1888.

WACKERNAGEL, W. *Altfranzösische Lieder und Leiche.* Basel, 1846.

WACKERNAGEL, P. *Das deutsche Kirchenlied.* Leipzig, 1864.

WATERWORTH, J. *The Canons and Decrees of the Sacred and Œcumenical Council of Trent.* London, 1848.

WERNER, R. M. *Lyrik und Lyriker; eine untersuchung.* In Lipps, Theidor, and Werner, R. M., Beiträge zur ästhetik. 1890–91.

WOODBERRY, G. E. *The Appreciation of Literature.* (Chapter II, Lyrical Poetry.) New York, 1907.

WORDSWORTH, C., and LITTLEHALES, H. *The Old Service-Books of the English Church.* London, no date.

WÜLKER, R. P. *Altenglisches lesebuch.* Halle, 1874.

THE COLUMBIA UNIVERSITY PRESS

Studies in English

Joseph Glanvill. By FERRIS GREENSLET, Ph.D. Cloth, 12mo, xi + 235 pp. $1.50 *net.*

The Elizabethan Lyric. By JOHN ERSKINE, Ph.D. Cloth, 12mo, xvi + 344 pp. $1.50 *net.*

Classical Echoes in Tennyson. By WILFRED P. MUSTARD, Ph.D. Cloth, 12mo, xvi + 164 pp. $1.25 *net.*

Sir Walter Scott as a Critic of Literature. By MARGARET BALL, Ph.D. Paper, 8vo, x + 188 pp. $1.00 *net.*

The Early American Novel. By LILLIE DEMING LOSHE, Ph.D. Paper, 8vo, vii + 131 pp. $1.00 *net.*

Studies in New England Transcendentalism. By HAROLD C. GODDARD, Ph.D. Paper, 8vo, x + 217 pp. $1.00 *net.*

A Study of Shelley's Drama, "The Cenci." By ERNEST SUTHERLAND BATES, Ph.D. Paper, 8vo, ix + 103 pp. $1.00 *net.*

Verse Satire in England before the Renaissance. By SAMUEL MARION TUCKER, Ph.D. Paper, 8vo, xi + 245 pp. $1.00 *net.*

The Accusative with Infinitive in English. By JACOB ZEITLIN, Ph.D. Paper, 8vo, viii + 177 pp. $1.00 *net.*

Government Regulation of the Elizabethan Drama. By VIRGINIA CROCHERON GILDERSLEEVE, Ph.D. Cloth, 8vo, vii + 259 pp. $1.25 *net.*

The Stage History of Shakespeare's King Richard III. By ALICE I. PERRY WOOD, Ph.D. Cloth, 8vo, xi + 186 pp. $1.25 *net.*

The Shaksperian Stage. By VICTOR E. ALBRIGHT, Ph.D. Cloth, 8vo, xii + 194 pp. $1.50 *net.*

Thomas Carlyle as a Critic of Literature. By FREDERICK W. ROE, Ph.D. Cloth, 8vo, xi + 152 pp. $1.25 *net.*

Leigh Hunt's Relations with Byron, Shelley, and Keats. By BARNETTE MILLER, Ph.D. Cloth, 8vo, vii + 169 pp. $1.25 *net.*

The Authorship of Timon of Athens. By ERNEST HUNTER WRIGHT, Ph.D. Cloth, 8vo, ix + 104 pp. $1.25 *net.*

English Tragicomedy. By FRANK HUMPHREY RISTINE. Cloth, 8vo, xv + 247 pp. $1.50 *net.*

The Rise of the Novel of Manners. By CHARLOTTE E. MORGAN, Ph.D. 8vo, cloth, ix + 271 pp. $1.50 *net.*

John Dennis. His Life and Criticism. By HARRY G. PAUL, Ph.D. 8vo, cloth, viii + 229 pp. $1.25 *net.*

LEMCKE & BUECHNER, AGENTS
30–32 WEST 27th ST., NEW YORK

THE COLUMBIA UNIVERSITY PRESS

Studies in English

The Middle English Penitential Lyric. By FRANK ALLEN PATTER-SON, Ph.D. 8vo, cloth, pp. ix + 203. $1.50 *net*.

The Exemplum in the Early Religious and Didactic Literature of England. By JOSEPH ALBERT MOSHER, Ph.D. 8vo, cloth. $1.25 *net*.

The Political Prophecy in England. By RUPERT TAYLOR, Ph.D. 8vo, cloth, pp. xx + 165. $1.25 *net*.

New Poems of James I of England. By ALLAN F. WESTCOTT, Ph.D. 8vo, cloth. $1.50 *net*.

The Soliloquies of Shakespeare. By MORRIS LEROY ARNOLD, Ph.D. 8vo, cloth. $1.25 *net*.

Thomas Dekker. A STUDY. By MARY LELAND HUNT, Ph.D. 8vo, cloth. $1.25 *net*.

Studies in Comparative Literature

Romances of Roguery. By FRANK WADLEIGH CHANDLER, Ph.D. In two parts. PART I. The Picaresque Novel in Spain. 12mo, cloth, pp. ix + 483, $2.00 *net*.

A History of Literary Criticism in the Renaissance. By J. E. SPINGARN, Ph.D., Professor of Comparative Literature, Columbia University. 12mo, cloth, pp. xi + 330, $1.50 *net*.

Platonism in English Poetry of the Sixteenth and Seventeenth Centuries. By J. S. HARRISON, Ph.D. 12mo, cloth, pp. xi + 235, $2.00 *net*.

Irish Life in Irish Fiction. By HORATIO SHEAFE KRANS, Ph.D. 12mo, cloth, pp. vii + 338, $1.50 *net*.

The English Heroic Play. By LEWIS NATHANIEL CHASE, Ph.D. 12mo, cloth, pp. xii + 250, $2.00 *net*.

The Oriental Tale in England in the Eighteenth Century. By MARTHA PIKE CONANT, Ph.D. 12mo, cloth, pp. xxvi + 312, $2.00 *net*.

The French Influence in English Literature. By ALFRED HORATIO UPHAM, Ph.D. 12mo, cloth, pp. ix + 560, $2.00 *net*.

The Influence of Moliere on Restoration Comedy. By DUDLEY H. MILES, Ph.D. 12mo, cloth, pp. xi + 272, $1.50 *net*.

The Greek Romances in Elizabethan Prose Fiction. By SAMUEL LEE WOLFF, Ph.D. 8vo, cloth, $1.50 *net*.

LEMCKE & BUECHNER, AGENTS
30–32 WEST 27th ST., NEW YORK